ADVANCE PRAISE FOR

TOMORROW
WAS YESTERDAY

This book is essential. In compiling these stories, Dede Ranahan has given us a profound and moving portrait of the world we mothers of those with mental illness live in. It is difficult for others to understand, or even believe, the tragic situations we contend with. It is time for the mothers, and other loved ones, to tell their stories loudly and with clarity, and this book does exactly that. I am confident these stories will cause the world to wake up, take notice, and implement the change we so badly need.

—MIRIAM FELDMAN,
painter and author of He Came In with It:
A Portrait of Motherhood and Madness

The written accounts in *Tomorrow Was Yesterday* are funny, sad, devastating, and heartbreakingly recognizable. I see myself, my parents, my grandparents, my sisters, and my daughter on every page. Reading these intimate accounts will change you. It changed me. And I hope it brings about the change—so desperately needed—to repair a system that has failed families for too long.

—STEVE GOLDBLOOM,
Emmy-nominated writer, producer, director, and creator of the
Brief But Spectacular series for PBS NEWsHour. The show's
mission is to invite viewers to walk in someone else's shoes.

The stories in *Tomorrow Was Yesterday* are a chorus of primal screams from mothers crying out for human decency for their family members. They take the leap to be vulnerable and transparent about their experiences in order for others to comprehend so changes can be made. If these stories can't convince policy makers, I don't know what will.

—MINDY GREILING,
Minnesota legislator for 20 years, and author of Fix What You Can: Schizophrenia and a Lawmaker's Fight for Her Son.

TOMORROW
WAS YESTERDAY

TOMORROW WAS YESTERDAY

*Explosive First-Person Indictments
of the US Mental Health System–
Mothers Across the Nation Tell It Like It Is*

DEDE RANAHAN

WITH 64 CO-AUTHORS

Tomorrow was Yesterday: Explosive First-Person Indictments of the US Mental Health System—Mothers Across the Nation Tell It Like It Is

For information about this title or to order other books and/or electronic media, contact the publisher:

Read First Press
PO Box 1187
Lincoln, CA 95648

Library of Congress Number: 2020916499

ISBNs:
Print: 978-1-7329745-2-4
eBook: 978-1-7329745-3-1

Printed in the United States of America

Cover and Interior design: 1106 Design

For the Mothers Everywhere

*My beloved son has severe paranoid schizophrenia. He's 22.
I live in New Zealand, where there are no facilities to help him.
He's made to have monthly injections as he has no insight into his
illness at all. He also has terrible drug and alcohol abuse issues,
and I'm his only support as no one wants him around. I found
www.soonerthantomorrow.com last night when I was feeling so
hopeless and I read all night—every story—and cried my heart
out. I just wanted to thank all of you because I really, really needed
you, and you are what helps in the dark times.*

Also by Dede Ranahan

Sooner Than Tomorrow
A Mother's Diary About Mental Illness,
Family, and Everyday Life

Winner: 2019 Nautilus Book Awards—Gold

Nautilus Book Awards Author Spotlight
Video/Dede Ranahan
https://vimeo.com/422993030

Finalist: 2019 Book Excellence Awards

Finalist: 2017 New Millennium Writings
43rd Literary Awards

Finalist: 2016 San Francisco Writer's Conference
Memoir Contest

Finalist: 2016 Writer's Digest Writing Competition

www.soonerthantomorrow.com
A Safe Place to Talk About Mental Illness in Our Families

*Carnations are the official flowers of Mother's Day.
Different colors have different meanings.*

Yellow carnations represent dejection and sorrow.

DISCLAIMER

The mental health information shared in these stories should not be taken as advice or recommendations. Every person and situation is different. If you or one of your family members are in need of mental health/illness assistance, please consult professional providers.

Our siloed mental health system can be difficult to navigate, and resources are often limited. Seek out advocates and advocacy organizations to help you find appropriate doctors, therapists, medications, information, and social and legal services.

CONTENTS

TIMELINE
MENTAL ILLNESS CARE IN THE US

1843: Dorothea Dix petitioned the Massachusetts Legislature to support the expansion of the state insane asylum in Worcester.

1907: Indiana was the first state to enact a sterilization law to prevent procreation of confirmed "criminals, idiots, imbeciles and rapists."

1936: The first prefrontal lobotomy was performed.

1938: Electroshock therapy was introduced as a treatment for people with schizophrenia and other mental illnesses.

1946: The National Institute of Mental Health was established.

1963: President John F. Kennedy signed The Community Mental Health Act, but it was never adequately funded.

1965: Medicaid's Institutes for Mental Disease (IMD) Exclusion prohibited federal funding for people in "institutions for mental diseases."

1967: In California, Governor Ronald Reagan signed the Lanterman-Petris-Short Act, which made involuntary hospitalization of people with serious mental illness (SMI) much more difficult.

1980: President Jimmy Carter signed the Mental Health Systems Act to improve services for people with SMI.

1981: President Ronald Reagan signed the Omnibus Budget Reconciliation Act, which repealed Carter's legislation.

2010: The Treatment Advocacy Center estimated that 50 psychiatric beds per 100,000 people would meet the needs of acute and long-term care, but in some states, the number of beds available was as low as five per 100,000 people.

2014: The Treatment Advocacy Center estimated that ten times as many people with SMI were jailed or imprisoned as were hospitalized.

2016: President Barack Obama signed the 21st Century Cures Act, which included the Helping Families in Mental Health Crisis Act.

2020: One-hundred-seventy-seven years ago, Dorothea Dix fought for humane care for the seriously mentally ill in the US. One-hundred-seventy-seven years of tomorrows later, their needs have not been met, and their numbers keep increasing.

Introduction

The Ask

One-hundred-seventy-seven years ago, in 1843, Dorothea Dix had a meltdown. A reformer and champion for the mentally ill, she argued passionately for better treatment and improved living conditions. So far, her vision—through no fault of her own—has turned, mostly, into 177 years of "We'll take a look at this issue tomorrow." As a result, the status quo of our national mental health system is untenable. I can't imagine what a worse status quo might look like. Millions and millions of individuals with serious mental illness (SMI) and their families are suffering, horrendously, every single day. The SMI community is overwhelmed, isolated, ignored, and out of patience. Time's up America. Tomorrow's good intentions no longer suffice. The way I see it, tomorrow was yesterday.

My son, Pat, died unexpectedly, July 23, 2014, in a hospital psych ward. In my book, *Sooner Than Tomorrow—A Mother's Diary About Mental Illness, Family, and Everyday Life,* I wrote:

I could write more about the last few weeks of Pat's life, my frustration and anger with our mental illness system (there is none), and the drastic need for change—sooner than tomorrow. I'd make a case for effective, compassionate care for our seriously mentally ill. I'd point out tragedies that could have been prevented and the urgent need for beds and housing. I'd challenge outrageous HIPAA laws that prevent moms and dads like me from giving and receiving lifesaving information. I'd talk about our missing and homeless children and mothers and fathers. I'd tell stories about our sons and daughters in jails and prisons and solitary confinement without treatment, and on and on . . . My writing would turn into a tirade, and that rant is for another time. Not here. Not on sacred ground.

Well, guess what. Six years later, "another time" is here. And now, I'm joined by a cadre of mothers from across the nation. Other mothers like me who want to tell our stories. Where and how did I find and connect with them?

On July 15, 2016, almost two years to the day Pat died, still grieving and needing *to do something*, I posted the first entry on my blog, www.soonerthantomorrow.com—A Safe Place to Talk About Mental Illness in Our Families. I wrote:

Please know that I intend this blog to be about more than me and my book. I want it to be a safe place for mothers and grandmothers and sisters and daughters—any family member or caregiver really—to tell our stories and share our insights about how to live our lives to the fullest, while trying to help someone we love cope with serious mental illness.

Here we go. Let's see where this takes us.

With that first post, I invited mothers (and fathers) to send me their stories. At the same time, I reacquainted myself with Facebook and found there were/are multiple serious mental illness (SMI) support groups up and running. I joined half a dozen and began reading the entries. The writers didn't have publication in mind. They were simply mothers (and fathers) sharing their feelings, doubts, frustrations, and outrageous situations. They were seeking empathy, advice, and camaraderie, and pleading to be heard.

I approached a few, asking if I could share what they'd written on my blog. I said I'd do some editing, if necessary, promising not to post anything until they'd reviewed my edits and approved of them. Trust had to be my gold standard. If I squandered someone's trust, I could toss my blog into the iCloud trash.

So we started, and week after week the stories began to add up. And the more of them I published, the more impressed I was with the mothers. From their collective revelations a dark opus emerged, and behind-the-scenes traumas and tragedies—endemic to the US mental health system—took center stage. The outpourings were not bureaucratic summaries or committee reports or statistical compilations or publicity-driven commentaries. The outpourings were screams from the depths of battered souls. As one of the moms, Nikki Landis, wrote when I asked to share her entry in this book, "I didn't write my posts to be public so they aren't very polished, I guess. But if something I wrote can help someone else, use it."

That's what I love about these stories They're honest, direct, unpretentious, and brave. In the selected snapshots from ongoing sagas (2016 to the present), you'll read about grim realities—terrible group homes, suicides, adult children killed by police, incarcerations and solitary confinement, lack of beds, family chaos, substance abuse, ineffective medications, "dying with their rights on," heartbreaking HIPAA restrictions, hallucinations, homelessness, sorrow, sadness, hurt, and anger. Simultaneously, you'll read about profound love, caregiving, gratitude, forgiveness, hope, strength, persistence, resilience, generosity, leadership, courage, advocacy, pursuing dreams, understanding, and fighting for change.

Here's the pitch. The ask. We want you, first and foremost, to read our stories. Set aside any conscious biases about serious mental illnesses and the people and families who struggle with them. Imagine us as relatives or friends—people you care deeply about. Pick up *Tomorrow Was Yesterday* and settle in for the next couple of hours. Kick off your shoes and slip into the worn-out shoes we mothers wear. Try them on for size. See how they feel. Are they comfortable? Do they cause pain?

If you read every story, and if you've not had personal or family experience with SMI, I guarantee you'll be a different person than you are right now. You'll entertain new thoughts and ideas about our mental health system. You'll wish us well in our efforts. You'll identify something you can do, in your own life, to help us prevail and obtain the mental health/illness care we desperately need.

And if you're another SMI mom reading *Tomorrow Was Yesterday*, trust me. Wherever you are, I'm confident you're going to feel less alone.

Please. Begin. I'll rejoin you after the last story, and we'll talk some more.

—DEDE RANAHAN
July 23, 2020

OUR VOICES

If one is mentally out of breath all the time from dealing with the present, there is no energy left for imagining the future.

—ELISE BOULDING

You Don't Matter &
There's No Limit to What a Mother
Will Do

—TERESA A.

Imagine having a problem, a medical problem. You go to the doctor. The doctor says, "I can't help. I don't understand what's wrong with you."

So off you go to a specialist. Surely the specialist can help. The specialist takes his time, talks to you a bit, and gives you meds. "These meds," he says, "will help. Maybe."

So you take those meds. The meds don't work. In fact, they make you worse. So off you go back to the specialist. This is where it gets fun. The specialist says, "Well, I'm not surprised you got worse. That's a side effect. Let's give you meds to counteract the side effects." Here's the best part. The supposed specialist then says, "I really can't diagnose you for about ten years. I'll give you different meds during that time and hope one might work."

At this point, you're so sick you can't make medical decisions. If you're lucky, you have someone to advocate for you. Oh, and did I mention that your friends and family don't call to see if you or your caregivers are okay? They think you simply need to shake it off and your caregivers are doing it all wrong.

After years of medicines that have destroyed your body, after years of hope that you'll get better, you have to wonder why you keep trying. You're now alone and still getting sicker. That diagnosis, the one that was promised long ago, is still elusive. Was your recovery ever really going to happen? Did all those specialists kick the can down the road while raking in tons of money?

Finally, when you're at your sickest, you're put in handcuffs, loaded into a cop car, and taken to a hospital. The hospital staff doesn't help you either. They give you different meds, ignore you for ten days, and send you home. You don't have cancer. You don't have heart disease. You don't have lupus. You don't have diabetes. You have a serious mental illness and you don't matter.

After six years at one not-for-profit practice, my son hasn't been diagnosed properly. He's not getting any better. He sees a nurse practitioner, not a doctor, for 20 minutes every two months. She consults a psychiatrist who has never met my son to make medication decisions.

So, we waited eight months to get an appointment with a psychiatrist in a practice that calls itself "neurological associates." We finally saw this doctor and told him, "We want help. We want a diagnosis. We want testing." The doctor sent for my son's records and we returned today. The doctor said to my son, "You have a chronic disease, most likely schizophrenia. I really can't help you, but I'll continue to see you if you want me to."

My son is mentally ill, not stupid. My son was excited to go to this appointment. He thought he'd get help and the voices might go away. My son is devastated. He says, "See, no one wants to help me." My son, obviously, doesn't want to go back.

The doctor says, "I'll see your son again if you want me to, but isn't this a far ride for you?"

I am sad and angry. What doctor tells someone they have a chronic disease but, "Sorry, I can't help you"? He also said,

"There's no testing for your son. No hospital here will take him off all his meds and try to diagnose him."

I'm angry but not surprised. Today is our 25th wedding anniversary. My husband's sad. We hugged and he went to bed. No celebrating here.

THERE'S NO LIMIT TO WHAT A MOTHER WILL DO

My father told me, "No one said life was fair,
Put a smile on your face cause the world doesn't care.
Our family's there to help you through."
I found out that this isn't true.
I wish they'd help—an ear to listen, a heart to care.
They can't understand mental illness from fear.
Fear that it's in their blood and, if it's true,
It can happen to their children, too.
So they blame me, my husband, my son.
It must be something that we have done.
I struggle alone to understand the disease you can't see.
I wish for the person my son used to be.
I'll do anything, fight anyone, learn all I can,
I wish I'd known when this illness began.
I could have helped my son sooner, maybe.
I should have listened to the mother in me.
There are days I cry for the future I dreamed he would live.
I cry because sometimes I think I've given all I can give.

I cry because I'm loving a boy who can hurt me so,
Feeling guilty because I can't take more, I want to let go.
Then the days happen when I see him once more,
The son with the gentle soul I adore.
He will fight this fight and I will, too.
There's no limit to what a mother will do.
My world has become all about this disease,
Praying to God to help him, please.
Tomorrow's another day and I fear how it will go,
I have painfully learned that I never know.
Some day I believe we'll rise from this storm,
Until then I'll fight, and I will be strong.

"MOMMY, PLEASE CLEAR MY NAME"

—HOLLY ALSTON

My son Terrell Anthony Scott suffered from schizophrenia and other mental health issues. At the age of five, Terrell tried to hang himself.

Terrell was incarcerated at Northampton County Prison located in Easton, Pennsylvania, from 2009 to 2014 without having a warrant against him, and no jurisdiction either.

The prison medical team ignored Terrell's mental health issues. They ignored Terrell's cries when he was being raped, beaten, bullied, and asking for medical treatment for being exposed to another prisoner's HIV infected blood. Terrell's pleas to go to trial were all ignored.

Terrell was accused of sexually assaulting three girls, punching their faces repeatedly, striking their teeth with a claw hammer (not one tooth was damaged), and a list of other horrible crimes.

While in Northampton County Prison, Terrell tried to take his life. He ended up on life support for overdosing his medication with his saved saliva. It took Terrell over four weeks to save up enough saliva to kill himself.

Terrell then spent two and a half years at State Correctional Institution at Retreat located in Hunlock Creek, Pennsylvania.

During his incarceration at SCI, Terrell tried to take his life again. He swallowed two razor blades, then took another razor blade and cut his neck from ear to ear three times and cut both his wrists, up to his forearms, 12 times. Again, Terrell's mental health issues were ignored.

Terrell did not commit the crimes he was accused of committing. This is how I know:

1. During the time Terrell was around the said victims, two Easton children and youth caseworkers came to the house twice a week. They made no mention of any form of abuse.
2. At school, neither the girls' teachers, the school nurse, nor the guidance counselor made mention of any form of abuse.
3. Mandated workers at the summer nights program, which a pastor ran, made no mention of any form of abuse.
4. My former boss, who is a hairdresser, saw the girls. They made no mention of any kind of abuse.

Terrell endured several years being away from his family, his only support system. He was held down by other prisoners while one inmate beat Terrell's head repeatedly, and suffered permanent hearing loss and loss of eyesight. He was paraded around naked at Northampton County Prison and thrown in the hole for months because other inmates lied about him. The list goes on.

Terrell completed his incarceration on August 8, 2016. He was registered as a sex offender under Megan's Law, and put on special probation requiring him to pay for lie detector tests on a monthly basis. All the while, his mental health issues weren't being addressed.

On August 20, 2016, Terrell took over 60 pills to kill himself. When his body rejected all those pills, he put a garbage bag over his head, secured it around his neck with jumbo rubber bands, and suffocated to death. Terrell's little brother, Amari, found him early that morning (the worst day of my life), but it was too late.

Terrell first asked me way back on December 26, 2009, "Mommy, if anything should happen to me while I'm in prison, please clear my name." He said this right before he got beaten up. Over the years, while Terrell was incarcerated, he would ask me to do the same thing, again and again. Terrell's last plea was to help clear his name.

I still haven't recovered from my beloved, late son Terrell being in prison for over seven years. I suffered a heart attack and a stroke from the stress of having a son in prison. It impacted my younger sons' lives. They grew up without having their older brother around. It changed us forever. Terrell was 30 years old when he died. He made a goodbye video two days before he took his life https://www.youtube.com/watch?v=yyhb_c-lD6o&feature=youtu.be.

My name is Holly and I'm desperate to get my beloved son's story out. Hoping someone can help me.

Terrell's last letter to his mother:

August 19, 2016

Dear Ma,

Hello, I just want to say goodbye. I love you sooooo MUCH! I can't live this life anymore. I HATE what my life has become. Crystal and the girls stole my life from me when they made all those lies on me. Now the world hates me. I can't allow myself to live anymore and see you struggle just to support me. I am ending my life so you can be free of me. Now Amari can move back in and help you. I made a goodbye video for you and everyone else that I love. It is on my phone. I left my info for my new Facebook and my Instagram pages. You are my everything. I don't want you to be sad or hurt because of what I am doing. I love you. Goodbye.

Love always, Terrell (aka Terry)

LOSING MY CHILD
BARBARICALLY

—MARGIE ANNIS

My child Ron was a 30-year-old man who still called me "Mama." Several hours before his death, he said to me, "I can do this on my own. I'm a grown man. Love you, Mom."

How to begin this story has been a struggle. My son died at the hands of our broken criminal justice and mental health systems. These systems are made up of people who have their own self-interests and who are discriminatory, indifferent, and ignorant. The man who was in, or who still is in, law enforcement was the vessel of this imperfect world and pulled the trigger. Victims. So many victims. My son is a victim and those who knew and loved him are victims.

The grief from losing a child is a roller coaster. So many what ifs and should haves as a mother who loves her child. All I wanted for him was to be good and happy in life and he was, when not afflicted with mental illness.

Ever since my son was killed by an off-duty detention deputy in Florida, I've been searching for the hows and whys of his life ending so tragically. Every parent's nightmare for a child who is afflicted with a serious brain disease came true for me—a disease my son was born with through no fault of his own.

Because of HIPAA privacy laws, I had to get Ronnie, my son, to sign a release statement so I could access his records to try to understand what was wrong when he was involuntarily committed in July 2012 in Florida. I had called the police because I had no idea where to turn to get help. I was unknowledgeable about the signs and symptoms of mental illness. My son was seeing things that were not there, believing the FBI, CIA, and Coast Guard were watching him from the sky with helicopters and drones.

Now I understand it was first episode psychosis.

It's amazing. When someone has a heart attack, is in a car accident, or breaks a leg, help is easily accessible. But when a loved one has a brain disease, there are no signs advertising schizophrenia or mental disease care centers.

I knew my son was mentally ill and had a drinking and drug problem as well. For months before he died, I made phone calls to rehabilitation facilities to try to find a place that would take a dual diagnosis individual ($30,000 a month or more). We were not wealthy, and money was a huge problem. I spent hours on the phone looking into intervention companies as well. My son could not understand or comprehend how sick he was. He had grandiose tendencies.

The last week of my son's life was sheer hell. I took him to a psychiatric hospital after a fiasco in the probation office. I was attempting to get him transferred to Alabama, where I live, and where we had help lined up. (He got into a fight with his brother in November 2015 in the front yard. When police showed up, Ron went berserk and was charged with domestic battery and resisting with violence. Can you believe it? Brothers fighting.) When I got my son to the psychiatric hospital, I was informed it was a for-profit facility and the cost would be $1500 a day. Ron refused to stay and he couldn't be forced.

I was sitting in our truck with my son and calling the Florida Mental Health Department to make an appointment for a mental health evaluation. There was a two-month waiting list so I called a private psychiatrist and got an appointment the following week. A probation officer said, "You could take him to an emergency room." This is one of those should-haves I didn't do. My thinking, at the time, was in an emergency room you wait and wait. It's triage and my son was not bleeding and, in his state of mind, I suspected he wouldn't sit and wait. And, of course, he had no insurance. My son had lost his job.

A week before he was killed, I pleaded with my son to voluntarily commit himself. He was considering it. He asked me and I told him, "Yes, Ronnie, do it." He didn't. Fearing my son would do something to cause harm to himself because of his irrational talk and actions three days prior to his death, out of desperation I called the police to try to get him Baker Acted, which is an involuntary commitment in Florida. The police got to his apartment too late. My son had just left for Daytona Beach. The policeman called and informed me, if he didn't see the need to Baker Act him, he wouldn't do it. Judgment by police is superior to a mother's judgment. Later, I found out the police should have informed me that I could petition a judge to have Ronnie involuntarily committed.

After he died, I listened to the 911 calls and obtained the police investigation report. It was not an easy task—a lot of hoops to jump through. The morning my son left his apartment on a rampage, police had been in contact. They stated in their report he had no warrants and he didn't meet criteria to be involuntarily committed—a danger to self or others. They let him go. My son was belligerent with them and was looking for his Bible on the side of the road. Ronnie stated to the police it flew off his dash and out the window. It was almost time for the police shift to end. In my way of thinking, they simply didn't want to bother with my troubled son.

An hour later, my son was shot dead by an off-duty detention deputy who had no crisis intervention training. The man who killed my son stated in the investigation tapes: "I was confused about what to do. I have never been trained with this kind of stuff, you know. He hadn't really tried to hurt me, at that point, but I was still scared to death." On the news, the sheriff stated that the deputy was a professional and trained, and thank God his deputies were okay. What about my son? He was killed. Apparently, his life didn't matter.

My son's comment to the deputy, according to the deputy, was, "I don't know what you're doing. I don't want to kill you. Just let me go. Let me go."

As his mother, I knew my son. He would deliberately provoke and let the imminent events unfold. He was not comprehending this detention deputy pointing a gun, swearing, and screaming commands at him. At the time, my son had no weapon and wore a pair of shorts. There were no witnesses—a law enforcement individual and a dead man. In less than two weeks, justifiable homicide was ruled by the state attorney.

In the past, I had high regard for the judicial system and law enforcement. What happened to my son and how I was regarded changed my thinking. An internal investigation is investigating oneself. The state attorney is going to side with the uniform (law enforcement). It's a brotherhood. Solidarity has its benefits, but not when a wrong has been committed.

I attempted to find an attorney. None would take a stab at a case with no witnesses and the involvement of law enforcement. The deputy was not dual-certified. He only possessed a certificate as a correction officer from the Florida Criminal Justice Standards and Training Commission. He couldn't take law enforcement action on behalf of the county sheriff's office while off duty. Also, based on his off-duty status during the incident, the sheriff's office order of limited authority did not apply to the incident involving my son and a sergeant. Bottom line: The sheriff's office was off the hook and not responsible for what a lone off-duty detention deputy did. Therefore, there were no deep pockets to get money for lawyers. A lawsuit brought on my behalf was not economically feasible for law firms.

I didn't care about the money. I was after any kind of justice. My son didn't deserve to die. There was no report in the news of a tragedy on behalf of my son. All that was reported was that a bad man, a criminal, was shot. He wasn't a victim, nor were his mother, his brother, extended family, and friends. My son broke the law because he was in the midst of a psychotic crisis.

What other disease is there that society will justify killing someone because of their symptoms? My son committed a crime so he was punished with death. It doesn't matter beyond those circumstances. His being psychotic and my not being successful in getting help for him is irrelevant. The sheriff and state attorney wanted to close my son's case quickly. After all, one of their own did the killing. No improvements can be made when there is no proof of wrongdoing.

In my small part of the country, since my son's death, there have been several more mentally ill people killed by lethal force. I'm in contact with other parents who've lost children the same way as I have. The places and times are different but the stories are the same, and the tormented, agonizing pain of loss is the same. I will carry the burden of losing my child, barbarically, the rest of my life. You will see me smile and laugh but, under the surface, the heartache is constant. To help heal, I'll do all I can for the seriously mentally ill and their loved ones to prevent them from enduring the life I am living.

15

I Just Want My Beautiful Boy Back

—ANONYMOUS

I'll never forget that phone call—my son, Will, had jumped off a freeway overpass.

His illness began a while before, when he developed psychosis from using crystal meth. I kept trying to get him help, but it seemed like there was no help available. Police would respond when he was in psychosis and take him to the hospital or to jail—depending on the officer. He'd been picked up so many times for possession under the influence that he was finally sentenced to a dual diagnosis program.

The program was terrible. I'm sure they did fine with some illnesses but not with schizophrenia. There were no medical people on staff and it was run mostly by recovering addicts or alcoholics. Will was sentenced there by San Diego Probation and court to complete treatment. He tried to run away a couple of times but was returned to finish his sentence. Finally, when he couldn't take it anymore, he ran away and jumped off the freeway overpass.

As Winston Churchill once said, that was "the beginning of the beginning."

Will was in the hospital for quite some time due to his injuries and then was moved to a step-down care facility. While there, he started having psychosis again, and they kicked him out on a weekend with no aftercare plan. He ended up going to his father's house to stay until we found a placement for him. While there, he was in psychosis and thought his father was the devil and that he had to attack him before his father attacked him. That resulted in the police being called.

Will was going to jail with a broken back and a broken foot. It was awful. He was in a wheelchair with a back brace. They wouldn't let either one into the jail so he had to hop on his broken foot and try to climb to the top bunk with this broken back.

So many horror stories I could tell about that time—his cast being wet, not being seen to have some pins taken out. After much intervention, they kicked him out to the county mental hospital to wait for placement. He got much better care there, although it was just a warehousing situation. He was there four months and then was put into an IMD (institute for mental disease).

Now, Will is there awaiting trial for attacking his father. He attacked him with a butter knife. Out of all the sharp knives in the kitchen, that's what he grabbed. I think that goes to show his state of mind. Anyway, visitation in the IMD has stopped due to COVID-19. I feel very grateful and fortunate that that is where he is when so many are homeless or in jail for the crime of being mentally ill.

My son is pleading "guilty to assault by reason of insanity." His attorney thinks he has a pretty good case, but it's so hard to know. Currently, he's happy and doing well. We pray that he doesn't have to go to prison, but he may have to go to the state hospital for a while. I'm almost as afraid of that as I am of prison for him. For now, things are good. We talk on the phone and I send him cards. I'm trying to enjoy as much time as I can with Will—while I can.

I have no idea what the future holds, but for today, we're okay. I pray for a future for my son but have little confidence in the system. I just want my beautiful boy back.

HELPING MR. K

—APRIL

My brother, "Mr. K," (what he calls himself) was born with Down syndrome. In 1968, we didn't know there were three different kinds. At least I didn't. His was so mild that he wasn't diagnosed until he was about three years old. I remember being so jealous of him until I was about nine years old when he plunged a fork into my chest. I was pushing his buttons, typical older sister behavior. But that day I realized my poor brother wasn't in any position to participate in sibling rivalry.

Since then, I've always had a protective feeling toward Mr. K. My mother refused to put him in an institution, which was the norm back then. The recent introduction of antibiotics meant his lifespan went from an expected nine years to who knows how long. I went to college. I stayed sort of in touch. I went on with my life. Periodically I would receive strange postcards from my brother indicating he was in the CIA and his life was in danger. When I would call him to find out what it was about he would say he was joking. In his 30s, he jumped off some stairs thinking he could fly and shattered his leg. Because of my mom's strong determination, they didn't amputate and his bones miraculously healed back together.

I should mention that, all his life, Mr. K has pulled his hair out and has absolutely no ability to restrain himself with food. He will eat an entire pizza and drink a whole bottle of soda when left to his own devices. When my mother died somewhat unexpectedly at 78 (she hid her symptoms of lung cancer, and then got pneumonia on top of her chronic COPD, a smoker since the age of eight), an elderly cousin was sent in to tell me that I had to take my brother, that he could do a lot of things, but he couldn't live on his own. That was seven years ago. It's taken me this long to understand what the hell was going on. I wish I had discovered your blog sooner.

Mr. K was severely delusional, rushing around telling people his wife had been murdered in Ireland and on and on. He was shockingly inappropriate with my teenaged boy. We took him to the emergency room. A neurologist tested him. He said, "Go see a psychiatrist." My brother was in his 40s at this time. He glommed onto my husband, who is not a caregiver type. My husband finally gave me an ultimatum: "It's your brother or me."

I found Mr. K an apartment in a senior disability/independent living facility and started taking him to the local mental health agency. I kept thinking, eventually, someone would put him in a hospital setting and get him stabilized. I paid $800 for a Power of Attorney that was too complex to do its job. For two years, I applied for assistance through developmental disabilities and was turned down each time. The third time they wrote their reason was the diagnosis of schizophrenia. I called the mental health agency and asked if this were true. They said it was. For two years they never told me what we were dealing with. My brother took the bus and hitchhiked to his imaginary property and went missing for three days. His phone ran out of battery power. He stayed at a homeless shelter and didn't think to ask to use their phone. (My brother's IQ is 72.) Even more maddening,

I called that shelter and described my brother (a 300-pound man with Down syndrome is pretty obvious). They said, "No he isn't here," instead of "I can't tell you if he is here." He was there.

I called hospitals and morgues. Only the police tried to be helpful. They filed a missing/vulnerable report which Adult Protective Services tried to have removed. Why? Because he didn't qualify for developmental disability services. I privately met with a director of developmental services in my area. She assured me Mr. K would receive all of the same services through a parallel system offered through the Department of Social and Health Services. She said he would probably do well in an assisted living or adult family home setting. Oh, it would be so easy.

Earlier this year, my brother got in trouble for writing letters to a newscaster he believed was his wife. When security at the station told him to stop, he sent her a Facebook message telling her he was angry at her for reporting him. So that got him three days in the "lockup" and started on a course of medication, which, the moment he got out, he stopped taking. I was told, "Don't worry. If he stops taking the medicine or behaves dangerously, we will bring him back to lock up."

They never did and never will.

We were able to get a caregiver to spend three hours with Mr. K three days a week, but he just used her as a shuttle service. He continued exactly as before—living in filth, eating terrible foods, acting out his delusions. After several months of this, I asked the agency, "Why don't you work with the caregiver?" They said, "We didn't know he had a caregiver." (It was their recommendation that helped him get the caregiver.)

Mr. K began applying for credit cards, birth certificates, and Social Security cards, in his belief that he was an admiral with a different name born 20 years earlier. He also developed heart failure and could not consistently take his medicines or get to his appointments. The last straw was when the COVID crisis struck. He told everyone, "I'm immune." He hugged his 97-year-old neighbor as she kept saying, "We're not supposed to hug anymore." The mental health agency said they would "give him a call."

Besides having the mental illness, or partly because of it, Mr. K can't remember from day to day what he's been told/warned of/reminded to do, even if he were to be cooperative. I knew the call wasn't going to have any impact. Just like all the other "interventions." So I went to his place with my suitcase, planted myself in his apartment, and we hunkered down for the first three weeks. I gave notice at his apartment and he understood. But when the social worker talked to him, he said he didn't want to go to my house or to an adult family home. So she said she would have to file a report to Adult Protective Services. Not against the Facebook scammers getting him to send them money. Not to get him into a safer, healthier living situation, but to stop me from helping him. Because his natural reaction is to resist the bossy, older sister.

Well, I called the apartment manager and reversed the notice. Mr. K went to my house with me, where he is again driving my husband crazy, but at least he is taking his medicines (heart and psychiatric) right on schedule. He's lost 14 pounds (down to 325) and is exercising twice a day. My guardianship hearing is next week.

I wake up feeling the best I have in years, knowing Mr. K is supervised even though I have to do it. Keeping him busy all day is a challenge, but the moment I let up things go awry. The social worker has been looking for an adult family home for two months now. I'm not sure how anyone is going to be able to manage him. My days of thinking the government or bureaucrats or this adult-family-home system will provide the answer are over. We can't leave it to people collecting paychecks to care for our loved ones.

For Now I'm Thankful
Adam Is Alive

—AUDREY ADAMS AUERNHEIMER

We traveled, yet again, to another state for our son's court appearance on Tuesday of this past week. Adam has spent five months in the county jail. We've traveled the five-and-a-half-hour distance from our home eight times in order to support him in his desire to represent himself in court. Most of his court dates were postponed at the last minute.

At long last, he got his requested bench trial before the judge. Of course, our son's defense was scattered and unfocused, and he failed miserably. The judge ordered him to be released to our care, with mental health treatment. That is about the best outcome we could hope for, considering the broken mental health system. It's winter. We don't want Adam released to the streets. However, he'll have a six-month probationary period, during which time he can be returned to serve a two-and-a-half-year jail term on charges of harassment by phone, and breaking a no-contact order.

This is our third child who's been diagnosed with serious mental illness. Our two other children are deceased by suicide. My husband and I are tired. For now, I'm thankful Adam is alive. Thanks to those of you who are prayer warriors in this unfolding, seemingly never-ending drama. Only our strong faith keeps us moving forward. We have very low expectations for effective care through the medical or legal community. We're not trying to be negative. We're just well versed in the ineffectiveness of the system.

I'm Gonna Brag About My Son

—HARRIET B.

This afternoon I texted a friend to come over and pick up a bunch of my son's nice hand-me-down clothes for her son. This is a woman we used to carpool to school with. She's my sister's best friend and knows that we've had many difficult years, and that this year has been especially difficult. I don't know how much my sister has told her, but it's public knowledge that my son had to leave school (where her daughters attend) and is in a treatment facility (for bipolar disorder, anxiety, and substance abuse).

Anyway, she blew in and immediately began talking nonstop about where her daughter had been accepted to college, where all the people in their class were going to college, how well her next two children were doing, how her daughter should marry so-and-so, and how so-and-so's kid didn't get into Stanford even though he made a 35 on his ACT and had straight A's. Blah Blah Blah. She seemed nervous and uncomfortable.

There we were, standing over a table of my son's clothes, and she never once asked me about him. It was as if he's dead or worse, never existed. This woman knows me too well to have not said something. And then to go on and on about all the other kids.It was really bizarre.

I just keep telling myself that my son has dealt with more challenges than all these kids put together. So I'm gonna brag about my son, Thomas (he has a name). He's doing great on Zoloft. He's passed four of his five classes this semester. He hugged me over and over again during Christmas. He's more aware of his anxiety and is expressing his awareness of it more than ever before. He's talking to us about his substance use. He's participating in his medical treatment. He's as smart as any of those other kids.

Thomas is beautiful and loved and mine.

Letters From Solitary Confinement

—KATHY BAKER

I'm afraid my son, Travis, is dying. He's been in solitary confinement for six months. He thought a prison guard was the devil and punched him so they put him in solitary. He's serving a 10-year prison sentence for first degree attempted murder. He thought a friend, John, was Satan and stabbed him. Currently, he's in the California Health Care Facility (CHCF) in Stockton, California. Travis has been diagnosed with bipolar disorder. He experiences delusions and hears voices.

Solitary confinement is killing my son. After all this time, a social worker told me they still don't have his medical records and are not sure of his diagnosis or his meds. Travis tells me the meds they're giving him are not helping him. They just make him sleepy and he can't see or think. I drive seven hours every Sunday to see him for one hour. He's deteriorating week by week. I don't think anyone cares. My goal is to get Travis out of the prison and into a true hospital. How can I find someone to help him? I need a miracle.

Travis's recent letter to his sister:

> *It's good to hear from you. I'm still not doing good. But I know that that can change. I feel like I'm losing touch with reality. But*

I'm hoping to cope better. Writing you is difficult because not much has changed. I'm still trying to cope with being isolated. I know this is temporary and that helps.

I feel tired most of the time and I don't feel like doing anything. I haven't been reading because my eyesight is going bad. I feel hopeful things will get better. I have felt terrible. I feel like this isolation is killing me. I have a TV now but it's not very pleasant to watch.

I am having a hard time relaxing. I have a lot of anxiety about the future. I feel I've dug myself a deep hole and my life is over. The guilt I feel for coming to prison is catching up to me. I had a chance to do the right thing and I didn't. I actually wish John was the Anti-Christ so my prison sentence would not be in vain. I know that is selfish. Reality is hard to face. I have to remind myself that there are people now going home and I have a chance, too.

I'm not doing good. I saw Mom and Russell today. It was torture to not be able to communicate with them. Fear has got me in a grip so tight I can't fight to get out of it. I am so frustrated. Mom drives all this way to see me and it's like I don't even appreciate it. I almost don't even want to see her because of the state of mind I'm in. It's hard to talk, function, write, read. At least I have a radio and I can listen to the Christian Companion Channel. That cheers me up some.

I have no hope of getting better. I'm trying to think positive. But honestly I'm still alive. I don't think God wants me to die like this. If only I can think positive. And seek life. I'm afraid to be alone.

This letter is just complaining. I feel so bad for complaining about me. I'm fine. I have nothing wrong with me. I'm ok. You are a blessing. I'm going to be okay. I'm feeling better already. Putting things into perspective I have no worries. I've been a coward. Praise the Lord. I've been delivered. I am really feeling better. You're suffering broke the chains of my suffering. I see more clearly. I love you. You are precious to me. Thanks for your honesty. Even though I'm sad you're not feeling well. The Grammy's are on. Love you. Love, Travis.

Travis's recent letter to his mom:

Mom, I love you. I got your letter today. I looked up your scripture. I think I'm doing all right but I'm not sure. I forgot what its like to feel healthy. I'm sorry if I'm scaring you. I'm terrified. My mental health is poor. I don't know if I'm okay or not. It feels good to write you. I know I'm okay now. Thanks for your support.

No one talked to me today. The only instruction I had was when I went to shower. I need attention. I don't know what to say to these people to get their attention. I feel if I had someone to talk to I could work through my confusion. I am so overwhelmed by my time I have left to serve. I feel like I can't breathe. Isolation is killing me. It's really scary. My mind is very powerful.

I love you Mom. Take care. Travis

My seriously mentally disabled son, Travis Christian, known as CDCR# BB8099, has been suffering since August 2017 serving most of his first year in the prison system in solitary, known as *the hole.* He is kept in lockdown isolation 24 hours a day. The facility will continue to keep him in isolation until April 2018 when he'll be transferred to level 4 prison, the highest security.

My son is not a gang member (just a mentally ill California surfer boy type), has the mentality of a teenager, and he's 31. When he's not properly medicated or is allowed to go off his meds, he can react violently because he fears for his own life. Travis is losing his basic motor skills, reading, writing, talking, and eyesight from wrong medications and long-term isolation.

At his sentencing he was given the choice: stay in a hospital for a longer-term or in prison for a shorter-term. He was advised to take the shorter-term in the prison system, but the shorter term is turning my son into a vegetable. My prayer is that someone will help my son live the rest of his 10-year prison term in a mental hospital that truly rehabilitates mentally ill prisoners.

It's Kind of Like a Daily "Sophie's Choice"

—GWENDOLYN BARTLEY

I'm happy to report that Mike handled the wedding and after parties with great success. My parents accompanied me in taking Mike back to his group home yesterday, and unfortunately, they witnessed our reality there. The group home is rundown and dingy, which is the typical group home. We have been able to make Mike's bedroom nice as we have the freedom to decorate, clean, and make it his space. My parents also saw firsthand how quickly violence escalates among the young men living there. One beat the snot out of another on the floor as we entered the living room. For all those who say mentally ill people are not violent, come spend a day here.

This is not where or how I want my son Mike to live but I have no other options in order to protect my other children at home. I struggle with this every day of my life and battle that I'm sacrificing his quality of life to protect his siblings. It's kind of like a daily "Sophie's choice."

It is deplorable living for the children. The caregivers are mediocre at best. There are only a handful of these group homes available in the state and all are equally as terrible. Beds are limited and I'm fortunate to have this home only 30 minutes away.

I pray daily for another option to become available for Mike. Meanwhile, I walk a tightrope advocating for his living conditions and care. I don't want him kicked out or treated poorly because his mom complains too much.

No one wants a group home in their community, but people are shocked when they learn that I can't find another location for Mike. Please be open-minded about allowing more group homes in your community. I will go to my grave fighting for the improvement and quality of these facilities for children and adults who have already suffered enough.

NIGHTMARES IN THE DAYLIGHT
& 10 MYTHS MENTAL HEALTH OFFICIALS
TELL US ABOUT OUR KIDS

—TAMA BELL

Thinking about my son and all he's been through—serious mental illness, homelessness, jail (more than once), and in the last few years, incarceration in prison.

Every time he was jailed or imprisoned, I could be anywhere and I'd end up "seeing him." Each time I "saw" him, I'd stop in my tracks. I'd stare and struggle to get a better view of the young man I was sure was my son. One time, I had to turn my car around and circle the area to get a better view of the young man. A better view of "my son," who couldn't be released without the prison telling me.

I knew he couldn't be released but I turned the car around anyway. I had to. "It might be him. Oh, my God! It looks like him and I recognize that hat (sweater, pants, sneakers, walk—you name it)." I turned the car around in an unfamiliar parking lot—a parking lot with huge potholes. I felt like I was sinking into each big hole, possibly never getting out. "Who cares?" I said, because now I was almost positive this was my kid. I was going to find out how he was released from the county jail, and how he made it hundreds of miles from the prison (and I was thinking—having nightmares in the daylight—about those hundreds and hundreds of miles, and the time, the ungodly, long, endless amounts of time).

Am I healing, I wonder? Again, I'm passing "my son" on the street, stretching my neck, staring out my passenger side window. He looks up as I slow down. He looks at me like I'm crazy—crazy as I feel. His eyes are unrecognizable. And now I see why.

He is not my son, and my mind is playing cruel tricks on me.

10 MYTHS
MENTAL HEALTH
OFFICIALS TELL US
ABOUT OUR KIDS

1. He/she is better off in prison. At least you will know where he/she is.

2. He/she is "malingering," "manipulative," or "not worth the effort."

3. Maybe he/she is right about not wanting to take meds. (They often say this to shame parents into allowing the person to remain sick, by having the right to be sick as opposed to the right to be well.)

4. He/she is "hard to serve"—meaning easy to drop the ball.

5. Because of HIPAA, "I cannot talk to you" (implying they cannot remain on the phone to listen to our concerns, or that they cannot read our letters). All lies. There is no law that says they cannot listen.

6. In order to help your loved ones, they must be a danger to themselves or others; which actually means we have to wait until our loved ones become dangerous or commit a violent act before they will help.

7. He/she needs to become homeless or needs to hit bottom before they can be helped.

8. He/she does not qualify.

9. There is nothing we can do.

10. There is nothing you can do.

Stuck in Texas

—JOYCE BERRYMAN

Leah was born September 13, 1986. She was a miracle baby. I'd already given birth to three daughters and had my tubes snipped after the third. Later, my husband and I decided to reverse my operation. After one tubal pregnancy and a miscarriage, Leah arrived.

Leah had three teenage sisters to love and help care for her. Life was good. I gave Leah many advantages—private preschool, pre-K, and kindergarten. She struggled in math and reading so I hired a private tutor. Her grades in math brought up the suggestion to have her evaluated for possible attention-deficit/hyperactivity disorder (ADHD), but her father refused to let this happen. We divorced after her fifth school year.

In high school, Leah did okay. She loved music, took private lessons in voice, and performed with a music group. After high school, Leah attended community college, and worked at a supermarket. During her second year of college, things began to unravel. Her first relationship ended, she dropped her classes, and quit her job. She stayed at home and started talking to herself. She called her voices the "people who live in my head."

Even though I'd gone back to school and received a degree in paraprofessional/special education, I didn't see the warning signs. I asked Leah to see a doctor, with no success. When she finally begged to see a doctor herself, I took her to a hospital emergency room only to be told there were no beds. This was in Washington State. The ER staff handed me some valium and antidepressants. Leah threw the pills down the toilet, so we went back and they gave us more.

By this time, my whole family was trying to get Leah the treatment she needed. My sister lived in San Marcos, Texas. She told us about a community mental health service there that takes anyone, regardless of income or insurance. So, we headed for Texas. Once in Texas, Leah improved a lot. She worked in the bakery at a major supermarket for almost two years, never missing a day of work, often taking last minute shifts for other people. It was hard to think she was ill at this time. We were living with my two older sisters. My oldest sister has bipolar disorder and with her moods, along with Leah's car breaking down, things began to unravel again.

Leah left home on foot in 100 degree temperatures. She returned home with blisters that no one in their right mind could walk on. Another time she left for four months and lived in a tent 20 miles from San Marcos. This was in the winter. She tried to hold onto a job at McDonald's. Her boss wanted to help her and encouraged her to go home. It rains often in the hill country in winter, and some nights Leah tried to sleep sitting up in a plastic tub. McDonald's had a truck stop close by with a bathroom. She was so tired she locked the bathroom door and went to sleep on the floor. The next morning, the truck stop manager told her, "If you ever sleep here again, I'll have you arrested." Leah's little encampment alongside an I-35 access road was about a mile from the highway patrol office.

They told her she had to move to a campground five miles away to be legal.

The fear that dug into every fiber of my being was not knowing if my daughter was okay and, if she did come home, how would I protect her? My fear abated when a crisis intervention officer typed a letter on official police stationery saying that Leah was fragile, severely mentally ill, and needed to be held, if found, because she had to take medication.

When she did come home that spring, a judge signed an order that she was a danger to herself. Since then, she's been hospitalized twice. The second hospitalization was voluntary. She was on many meds that made her worse. Sometimes she'd slap herself until her face was red and swollen. Sometimes, she'd come out of a trance and say, "Mommy, it's not me, it's the voices." I'd try to hold her hands, but she'd ask me to move away because "my hands will bite you."

Now Leah's on monthly shots of Invega and is doing better. It will be a year in November. I have a lot to be grateful for. Her treatment team includes me in everything. Leah is on Medicaid and I didn't have to beg for it. It took a year, but she receives services for free, and Johnson & Johnson gave her the meds until Medicaid started.

We are a family working together to help Leah. She gets $470 a month from Social Security, which is not enough to be independent. Young people with serious mental illnesses are handed a huge financial problem. If they can't work, they never get a chance to pay into Social Security.

Everyone says we are so fortunate here in San Marcos. I agree, but we're also held hostage to a place where Leah can get help. San Marcos is away from home and expensive to live in. Half of our income goes to rent. Leah and I share a one bedroom apartment. The rent increases every year by $40. If we could afford to buy a car, I could work evenings but all my energy goes to my daughter.

We appreciate what we have, but I wonder what happened to all the promises for community services after de-institution-alization. I believe the federal government owes compensation to full-time caretakers who took over the jobs of hospital staff when they abandoned thousands of people and families. The cost in lives and unmitigated suffering is unknown by any records.

No One Asks.
She's Been Erased.

—RONNI BLUMENTHAL

We're new to this world. That's not to say there weren't signs or moments that made me wonder and then push away the thought. Middle school and our first counseling. It didn't seem to help.

The first months of high school and everything seemed fine. Mari went to football games and had friends. I was excited. Mari's brother had severe attention-deficit disorder (ADD) and other challenges and never participated in any school activity.

Then. First the self-harm, then the death of a dear cousin, and then the 72-hour stay in the adolescent psych unit. Meds, new school, counseling. Refused intensive outpatient. Grew sadder and sadder. In the new school, her "stirring of the pot" socially and setting one friend against another was soon recognized, and the initial welcoming and flurry of invitations and activities came to a near total halt.

Friendless, and without a sense of self, Mari invented herself a million different ways on the internet. Some were dangerous. She got sadder and more anxious. She stopped sleeping. She cried. She stopped going to school. We changed the medication and she fell down the rabbit hole, tumbling and tumbling until I could hardly see her at the bottom. As she happily peeled the skin off her lips, I coaxed her to shower, to move from the bed to a chair. Two and a half months later, she took off her toenails and no one had answers. Four weeks ago we brought Mari to a facility far from home, the best we could find.

Today, we took our family photo for Thanksgiving and, for the first time since she was two, Mari wasn't here. And no one asked. Oh, you could feel their knowing thick in the room—the in-laws, the family friends, the older nephews, and even her brother.

No one asked. She's been erased.

Mari doesn't have something we can talk about, like a life-threatening disease (but oh, it is, and it has been). She doesn't have a broken leg or a hip replacement. She's 15 and in a state a long way away and still sitting at the bottom of the rabbit hole, with little interest in reaching up.

At the end of the day, I received photos of my daughter with half of her smile on her face. A start. Another showed her cradling two tiny puppies recently born to the canine program. My baby. That hair. Those eyes. Who can I send the photos to? No one asked.

She called. We spoke for a few moments and her grandparents each spoke with her. Then it was over. Just like that.

The photo with the puppies, the way Mari's holding them against her chest, cupping the second one's head in the palm of her hand—that's where the spark of hope resides.

I will teach them how to ask. And I will tell them.

Between Now and the Next
Full Moon

—JUDY WALDO BRACKEN

Checking my calendar, I see that my next scheduled event is the full moon, over a week from today. Really? That seems impossible. Perhaps I've forgotten to write something down—an appointment, a phone call reminder, a volunteer commitment, or meeting. But no, it all seems to be in order.

I've been trying to clear my calendar for months, years really, and I never actually thought it would happen. Trying to clear it so that I'd be open for the next crisis, the next call from the hospital, the alert from the police, the doctor visit, or the call from my son talking in nonsense statements. Whatever it was, I needed to be unscheduled to avoid the disappointment of having to cancel my plans due to that ever present possibility of a crisis.

Why would I do this? Why do I feel I have to put my life on hold when someone in my family is not doing well? In looking deeper, I realize how unfair I'm being to myself. I am healthy and strong, independent, financially secure, with plenty of time on my hands. Instead of feeling free, I'm filled with a deep sense of emptiness. Empty nest, empty house, empty calendar. For some reason I've been conditioned to put my own sense of fulfillment aside until everyone in my family is happy and healthy.

It's time to put something new on my calendar. It's time to take an "about face" in my thought patterns. It's time to realize my own happiness is not so dependent on others. It's time to accept the new family paradigm that includes my mentally ill son as he is or may be with the proper help. It's time to realize that the challenges that turn our lives upside down and inside out can actually be experiences that strengthen and broaden us and our views of the world. It's time to draw from my own strength and to continue to fight for my son. It's time to be content with my life as things are right now.

The fall leaf colors in my backyard are indescribably beautiful. The dog snuggling next to me is soft and warm. My muscles are exercised from a vigorous swim workout this morning. I'm breathing and my heart is steadily beating. My calendar is empty, but there is plenty to do and think about between now and the next full moon.

A Problem Shared
Is A Problem Halved

—MARA BRIERE

In my case, I've come to the realization that, although very much impacted by serious mental illness in many of my family members, I rarely talk about what it looks like and feels like—to me. It is, of course, the biggest motivator toward my founding the organization, Grow a Strong Family, for family members to receive the information and support so desperately needed. I realize there's a healing power in sharing these deeply felt emotions and, as is taught in 12-step programs, a problem shared is a problem halved.

When I was five, my family moved from a veteran's development in Flushing, New York, to live in my grandparents' two-family house in Bayside, New York. This was a big move from a relatively crowded neighborhood to a quiet suburban community. My grandfather was retired and became a founding member of AA in Queens, New York. My grandma was manic-depressive (now referred to as bipolar) and in and out of the hospital. The move meant that my mom would take care of us (two little girls, five and nine) and her mother. It was the time when lithium was first introduced and little was known about it. The state hospitals were colonies where the very sick would live out their lives. In the middle were the occasional "regulars," like my grandma, who'd become too sick (manic and not sleeping for a week before plummeting to suicide attempts or immobility and staying in bed for weeks on end) and return home when stable only to return to the hospital as another episode would strike. It became our job to monitor grandma. We'd call Mom, who would have her hospitalized, and then grandpa would get her when she was ready to come home. Mom would visit; us kids rarely. Throughout this, we didn't talk about grandma or the impact her serious mental illness was having on us.

Fast forward. I went to college to become a social worker. Although my education has since taken many turns, the influence of my grandmother's suffering and the family silence left a deep scar in my soul. I wanted better services. I really wanted more efficient communication and understanding for our family. I wanted solutions that would support the whole family.

I danced around my calling, even with education, professional training, community work, and a strong focus on family, until my beloved daughter, Erika, was diagnosed with a serious mental illness at age 25. In the interim, other family members had been diagnosed and treated, but there had never been a conversation about symptoms or the impact on the family unless I brought it up.

My daughter and I were very close. She was a velcro child. She was sensitive, sweet, creative, bright, had a great sense of humor, and knew she was loved and supported no matter what. Ours was a bond I'd dreamed about since I was a child and wanted to be a mother. We had similar interests, played games together, went on trips, shared music, and enjoyed a convivial relationship. There were times, of course, when there were family issues, and our family addressed them openly and honestly. We knew how to ask for and receive help. For example, after graduating with her BA, it was hard for Erika to find work. We supported her need to be independent while managing depression by providing financial and emotional support. Even with all that, serious mental illness distorted our relationships, caused confusion, and tore us apart.

When she was first diagnosed, Erika relied on me in ways that had never been needed before. There was a plea to "help me understand." "Come to my med appointment with me." "Help me with graduate school." "Help me with my assignments." It was hard for both of us since we were assuming uncomfortable roles.

At the time, she had an awesome prescriber who was excellent at explaining the symptoms, the illness, and how to manage it. My daughter had a strong support system and the odds looked good for her recovering from her first manic episode with little negative consequence. However, she was also making medication decisions that prolonged her instability. During this period, she recognized that she needed more frequent therapy sessions, but her past therapist was unavailable. She needed me to help her find a new therapist, which I did, and I made sure to emphasize that the work needed to be around her diagnosis and how to manage it.

By the time she finally ended up on lithium, (to which she responded, "Why did I wait so long?") the nature of her therapy work changed and focused on historical family issues. Why any therapist would do this kind of work with an unstable client is beyond me. While my daughter was getting clearer, the focus was on rewriting the past and a rift grew between us. It went from, "I need space," to "I hate you! You've never kept me safe!" The "space" grew.

After six months, I started a campaign to reconnect by sending funny cards, postcards, cookies, and other care packages, but Erika emailed me and told me to stop. She said, "I hate your attempts to buy me off. Don't waste my time. I just throw everything away." So I stopped.

At another point, my husband, her dad, was in the hospital, and I texted her and her response was, "I don't care." A year later, her uncle died and I emailed her to let her know. Her response was, "Send my condolences. I really don't care."

In spite of all of this, I held onto the hope that she would stabilize and return. Her responses were very hurtful. I found myself alternating between extreme anger (retroactive abortion anyone?) to overwhelming compassion because I knew that, as much as I missed her, she had to miss me even more. I was always the "I'm here for you" person for her, and her illness pushed me away.

After a couple of years of silence, Erika defaulted on the student loans I co-signed on her behalf. I called her to see about resolving the loan issue. With no response, I decided to send her the things I held in storage for her. I didn't want her to lose her childhood mementos just because I sent them, so I used the name and address of someone she was in contact with as the return address. Oh, my. This caused such a ruckus. She took out a restraining order on me and dragged me to court to defend myself. That is when I found out she had changed her name.

When I first received the restraining order, I said to the officer, "It's very easy to stay away from someone you don't know." Alas. I brought a lawyer to court with me, and the order was vacated since there was no threat involved. As we left, my attorney said, "Stay away. No more contact. She's not safe for you." And I have. It's been two years since that incident and there's been no contact.

I think about Erika every day as I accept that, for her, this is what her illness looks like. She has no family support. She has no ties to her own foundation. Through her illness, she's morphed into a person I can't connect with and a way of being that is anathema to me. Yet, I miss the daughter I knew and loved. I grieve for her every day. I want her to find her way back to me. I don't know where she is, what she's doing, or how she's doing.

On the other hand, I still have much work to do as I'm the primary support and case manager for another family member with serious mental illness. It's an uphill battle. The work is difficult because models of care don't acknowledge serious mental illness or the lack of insight, resources, and ability.

I founded my organization because I needed to understand what was not being made clear to me as a family member. With so much focus on the identified client, the family system is ignored. The outcomes are much better for everyone when there's open communication, factual education, and an understanding of how to manage serious mental illness effectively.

Fighting for Change

—ALLISON BROWN

My story is pretty long and spans generations. My dad was sexually abused by an uncle beginning at the age of three until he was about 13. At age 17, this uncle died and my dad began having episodes of anxiety. In reality, my dad was experiencing manic episodes followed by severe depression.

By the 1980s, he married my mom and had three children. I was four the first time I witnessed my dad hallucinate. He was convinced my baby brother was a demon. He held him up by his feet and told my mother he had to kill him. My older brother escaped to a neighbor's house and called for help. I watched from a window as my dad punched my mother in the face. Police struggled to restrain my father and take him away. He went to Greystone Hospital in New Jersey where he was diagnosed as manic depressive.

My dad's "episodes," as we called them, happened many times throughout my young childhood. Most of them were violent, but only in the sense that he saw demons and was attempting to protect people from the demons.

In 1992, my dad had another episode. My parents were divorced, and my younger brother and I were spending the weekend with him. The visit was supposed to be supervised by my grandfather, but the family knew something was off. They told us to leave. I locked my brother and myself in a bathroom until my aunt arrived. Later that day, my dad called my mom to tell her my brother was a ghost. She persuaded my dad to bring us to my grandparents' house, where she met us.

We had one last Sunday family dinner. My grandmother made her famous sauce and everyone pleaded with my dad to go to the hospital. He refused. There was nothing anyone could do. The next day, he went back to my grandparents' house and asked to be taken to the hospital. My grandfather had one errand to run before he took him. He was gone 15 minutes. When he came home, he found my father foaming at the mouth standing over my grandmother's lifeless body. He shouted "The queen demon is dead."

My dad was found "not guilty" by reason of insanity and moved to the Greystone Psychiatric Hospital, where he spent over a decade. He was then released on what is essentially parole for the mentally ill. He first transitioned into living with my aunt and, eventually, into his own apartment, but his illness was not curable. He continued to cycle through episodes. He spent the better part of another decade at Ancora Psychiatric Hospital in New Jersey.

As I came into adulthood, I became an advocate for care for my dad. I also advocated for the court to keep monitoring him for his safety and for the safety of all around him. Many times doctors refused to talk to me because of the HIPAA law. They'd listen to the signs I was seeing then tell me, "He doesn't seem dangerous to us." In 2012, after six months of communicating with his doctor to no avail, the doctor called to tell me, "Your father body-slammed me, stripped himself naked, and ran down the highway." My father was eventually diagnosed with bipolar

III disorder and schizoaffective disorder. He spent another five years away. Our story is sad and complicated and layered. It scarred my family.

My older brother turned to drugs. He had six children by as many women, and was incarcerated for felony domestic assault. My husband and I adopted his youngest son at the age of nine, but we were too late. He had been so traumatized that he was unable to function in our house. We had intense in-home therapy for four years. The safety of my own children was paramount. My nephew was Baker Acted (involuntarily committed) in Florida four times in one month for suicidal ideations. One time, a deputy came to the house and told me, "You just need to handle him better. This seems like a family issue."

My nephew became violent in our home and was eventually removed in cuffs. The state did nothing to help us. The paper wrote a story about us. Nothing changed. Eventually, the court accepted our surrender of parental rights and put my nephew in a group home.

Our family has been knocked down so many times by the failures in the system. We have advocated for help. For change. For a better system. We've gotten nowhere. I believe families should have the right to discuss mental health issues with doctors and therapists, even if it goes against what the mentally ill person wants. I believe in continuity of care, from therapist to therapist, which rarely happens. I believe in better training for our officers, teachers, and hospital staff. I believe in common sense laws that could save lives and protect our mentally ill loved ones as well.

The Caregiver's Sadness

—KENDRA BURGOS

There's a sadness that gets into your bones. It climbs on your back and weighs you down, seeps into your lungs and clenches on to your every breath. It lays in the empty space your loved one should occupy. It's the dead air on the other side of a telephone line. It takes the song out of your voice, and the words out of your hands, making it taxing and difficult to get it on paper.

That is the sadness. If you've ever felt it, you know what I mean. If you've never felt it, I am happy for you. It comes once you've gotten too comfortable, when your shoulders start to come down, and you begin to feel like you can actually breathe again. This type of sadness doesn't just creep up on you, this is the kind that hits you like a brick and leaves you reeling, trying to find your bearings. It is the caregiver's sadness.

I don't have a mental illness but I live with it.
I am the wife of mental illness.
I am the mother of mental illness.

I have been silent for the last couple of weeks, so overwhelmed from the current state of events that have taken over our family.

The depths of my emotions are so cutting and deep it's hard to put into words. I am numb. I feel like the wind has been knocked out of me. I feel beat and broken. It's my own fault. When things are level, you have your everyday ups and downs and you take those good times for granted because it just becomes normal. You forget how bad it can get when your loved one is not well.

We know that life with mental illness is unpredictable. One day everything seems fine only to come crashing down on you the next. There are, of course, the signs that you're heading for imminent disaster, but by the time you begin to notice that something's off, oftentimes it's too late. The disease comes roaring at you like a lion. You're caught before you even had time to run. We are caught.

With mental illness, when things are good you start to get a false sense of security, you start to breathe a little easier. Hoping maybe this time everything will stay level and we can just be, but mental illness is cruel. It doesn't work like that. Eventually, it comes creeping through the door. Bipolar came pounding on the door. I begged you not to answer, but you let it in anyway. It took you far away and in your place left the madness.

We've been, for a long time, balanced and navigating the course. It lingers in the background, the mental illness. It's present in our lives but it's certainly not the focus of it. It's just a chronic condition that is managed with medication. Much like any chronic condition, you take your required medication, regularly check yourself to make sure you're on the right course, stay up to date with your doctor, live a heathy lifestyle, and that's it.

My husband's done well to keep it at bay. This isn't the kind of thing where he's non-med-compliant, or in and out of hospitals trying to find the right formula. He provides for the family and holds a job. He's a skilled worker. He knows his limitations, and I've done my best to protect him as well as I can from the everyday stressors and burdens. But it isn't enough.

You can help, offer advice, provide support, but you can't control someone else's thoughts and actions. You can't live inside someone else's brain to really see what's going on in there—how it processes information, or the reasons for what feels best for them. You can only trust that they'll make decisions based on the well-being of everyone, not just themselves. The mind can be deceptive, but a mind that's been overrun by mental illness is a battlefield of sorts.

We've been through so much together, things that can test the bounds of a relationship—loss of a parent, loss of dear friends, financial stresses, teenagers that question a faith they once clung to. We've ridden the storm with a sick child. We did that together. We weathered the seasons of change and the storms of our life together. Now, for the moment, it feels I am weathering this storm alone. I am fighting for him and he fights against me. In his delusion, I am the enemy, not trusting his judgment that he's okay. He is not okay. We are not okay.

How do you care for someone who doesn't think they are ill? Caught up in the grip of sickness, they believe they are fine. Blind to how far off course they've become. The ones closest, bending over backward to care for their needs, take the brunt of the abuse. For the moment, their world revolves around them as it rightfully should. They are sick. There's little appreciation, or recognition. Most of the work of the caregiver goes unnoticed, while the faults are laid bare.

As much as you want to place blame—they should have stayed on the meds, they should have said something sooner, they should have . . . It doesn't matter because you just have to deal with what's in front of you. You can't reason with someone who is not well. Your voice falls silent. Except you can't stay quiet. It is your job to be the voice of reason.

Your loved one is looking to you to be their voice. But in sickness they don't like what they hear. In wellness there are things that you discuss, an emergency preparedness plan of sorts. They ask, if you start to notice them doing this or acting this way (the red flags), that you say something. Do something. But sometimes it's just too late. He won't remember half of what was said and done when the mania ultimately subsides. I will be left to sort out what the madness has done in impulsiveness. He won't remember but I will. And love will cover that.

Anosognosia—#1 Enemy

—GG BURNS

It seems I have more friends with children who have suffered from a brain disease and are now free (passed), than friends with children who have figured out a way to recover.

My son has suffered for most of his life. Nothing was easy for him (or us—his family), even though he was bright and full of life and joy until his brain illness took over. We tried everything. Twelve long years of IEP (Individualized Education Program) special accommodations in the school system; special diets; special vacations (with as little stimuli as possible); special cocktails of meds (some worked, some made him worse, while others were like a miracle cure). For a while, in his late teens, the future looked good. He was adjusting and transforming into a responsible young man with enormous dreams.

Yet, as my son grew older, his desire to be normal, to be free of the labels and the "special world" we'd built for him became the enemy. He broke away from his life of special accommodations like an animal from chains. Once he was free of his chemical straightjacket, he refused to return. He was higher than a man on cocaine. The mania and impulsive, reckless life were what he wanted. In his world, he was king. He could now do anything and there were no rules or consequences. And even when his recklessness and abandonment met handcuffs, locked doors and bars, he didn't seem to notice, because it forced him to sink deeper into a total psychotic break from reality.

Over time, as my son's illness progressed, my own health declined. For almost 11 years I have battled PTSD, anxiety, and painful autoimmune diseases. My son is trapped in a place that is worse than death—the carousel of insanity, the revolving door that leads nowhere. It just keeps him from killing someone and then spits him back out to the streets—untreated.

We'd never treat a human being with Alzheimer's this way, yet the USA abandons the sickest people in our country every day to live in homeless shelters. The senseless system of "self-directed care"—a recovery bullshit model developed for addicts, but not for people with serious brain damage—forces people who are at their worst to hate their own parents. It keeps us from communicating with their medical providers even when they are hospitalized. Their medical providers are trained to tell our sons/daughters that we are the ones who made them sick. It's worse than death for many of us.

The more I try to help my son, the more determined he is to refuse treatment that would restore his sanity. He sadistically and verbally abuses me, and there is simply no way to have a conversation or to even meet in person. He calls and texts with extreme threats to end my life. I, in turn, go through extraordinary measures to have him committed and the state hospital kicks him out in less than three days. In this crazy "no-care" world we live in, it is all about his rights to refuse. I lay in bed at night wondering when will this ticking time bomb finally blow? I ask myself how many people will blame me for his death or blame him for mine?

My son is constantly angry about everything that he has not been able to do in his short life.

He blames his parents.

He blames the banks.

He blames doctors who diagnosed him years ago.

He blames the government.

He blames the hundreds of mental health providers who have "attempted" to provide him some small level of care in spite of the fact he doesn't believe he has an illness.

In my mind, my son's "anosognosia" (lack of awareness of one's symptoms) will always be the #1 enemy. We have gone to war with this debilitating symptom, making it a household name in our attempts to lobby for state/national parity and system changes that would require someone like my son to agree to treatment, in spite of the fact that they don't believe they are ill.

Until our civil liberty laws change, my son's brain will continue to deteriorate. It is a costly, unjust, and inhumane way to die. Brain disease and cancer are both treatable. Some recover, some don't. The difference is that patients with cancer usually realize they have an illness.

My faith and earth angels (friends who understand) help me realize I must take care of myself in order to be there for my son—even from a distance. I find comfort in painting, gardening, and supporting others. I fight with every determined ounce of life I have for legal policy changes that might breathe a longer life into my son and others like him before it is too late. I rest when I can. I pray. I weep.

I am the mother of a gifted young man who is surviving a serious brain disease called bipolar disorder in a world that allows him to die a slow painful death—untreated.

Note: GG died in 2019. Her son is still ill.

Let's Talk About Hopeful Voluntary Admissions

—MARY A. BUTLER

Let's talk about hopeful voluntary admissions. We have had four very long ER visits (5–14 hours each) in the last couple of months trying to admit my fear-filled, very psychotic son voluntarily. When my son gets to the point that he's asking to go to the hospital, he's beyond ill and fearful. He battles monstrous auditory hallucinations while he's in crowded waiting rooms with the elderly, sick babies, and patients with infectious diseases. It's horrid for him and potentially horrid for them.

No beds were available in the Philadelphia metro/suburban area within a 50-plus mile radius. These four useless ER visits led to exacerbated illness, resulting in an involuntary admission, which is always more heartbreaking and exhausting. Unfortunately, in our locale, we cannot call or look for available beds on our own. It must be done in a local ER as follows:

- Long waiting room wait.
- Triage evaluation (psych patients are rarely prioritized).
- Back to the waiting room and possibly another long wait.
- Med clearance including blood/urine tests.
- Psych evaluation by social worker when available.

- Insurance approval—usually a lengthy process.
- Bed search (typically hours/sometimes days).
- Clinical review/approval by the admitting facility if a bed is available.
- Wait for available transport to the admitting facility.
- Lengthy wait/intake at the admitting facility at whatever hour fatigued patient arrives.

At times, very ill patients have been known to lie in ER beds from overnight to an entire week-plus until a bed becomes available. How terrible that someone seeking mental illness treatment is left waiting so long. Imagine if this happened to someone with appendicitis or broken bones. Understandably, patients with serious mental illness become uncomfortable, frustrated, anxious, and further disturbed. They receive very little attention from ER staff unless they're acting out. Many, including my son, give up and walk out—of either the waiting room or the examination room. The process is much the same here for involuntary admissions. They involve the police, lengthy paperwork at the county crisis center, and legal approval. So tack on several more hours.

I've mentioned to several ER docs and nurses, to no avail, that these critically ill patients should have a separate waiting area, be triaged expeditiously to an ER bed, and not be left alone for long periods of time. It's a cumbersome and careless system. The entire process needs to be streamlined and more efficient. It needs to provide timely access to safe and attentive emergency care and in-patient beds.

The mainstream media paint the picture that if only these mentally ill individuals would seek/get the necessary help, then we wouldn't see these ongoing mass shootings. That may apply to a few, but truly no one, especially the media, has a clue as to the availability of mental health care, let alone timely/quality care, unless they've walked in our weary shoes.

Bottom line: We're serving our seriously mentally ill in a very questionable and trepidatious manner. The availability of inpatient beds is in crisis. It's no wonder. Several of the better hospital psych units in this premier healthcare area have closed (not profitable) in lieu of expanding profitable cardiac units. It's a crying and growing shame, leaving personal and community tragedies in the making.

It Feels Like the State of Michigan Wants Me Dead

—SARAH C.

I am at my wit's end. I can't take it anymore. I have a mentally ill son, Christopher, who will be 17 in February. I was a victim when I was 13, and he was born when I was 14. I read so much when I found out I was pregnant—everything that would tell me how I should have the baby and where there would be help. I thought I was doing the right thing. Fast forward. He's now at a residential treatment facility. Since he was seven or eight, my son's been receiving treatment for mental illness. It was a battle every day to make sure nothing made him mad, and when he did get mad, we followed safety plans to a "T."

Christopher has bipolar disorder, ADHD, intermittent explosive disorder, and possibly—and probably—more. When he gets mad, he physically assaults people and it happens out of nowhere. He's gone after his infant siblings, strangers in the street, classmates, and teachers. He will attack anyone who's around. He says, "I will kill everyone." His main desire is to stab people to death. He attempted to stab me. He hid in the house with a butcher knife my grandmother used and forgot to lock back up.

We've exhausted all mental health services, and I mean all. I even drove him out of state to be hospitalized. The residential treatment facility is the last thing that can help, but I can't afford it. Child Protective Services, therapists, other family members, and medical providers all agree he needs this, but insurance won't pay for it unless he is a drug user.

So here we are. All involved agree my son cannot be in my home. It's too dangerous for me and his younger siblings. He's strong and over six feet tall. I love him, but I'm deathly afraid of him. So are my two daughters, whom he attempted to sexually molest as well as physically assault. The state of Michigan would help me pay for his treatment, but here's the catch: I'm being charged with child abuse and child neglect. Authorities say it's the only way to keep everyone safe and to get him help. They've put me on a child abuse registry. I won't be able to go back to working with children (I previously worked in an elementary school). I can't go on field trips with my other children because my name is on that list.

My trial isn't until January 10, 2019. The attorney they assigned to me doesn't seem to care about my right to a fair trial. He's only showed up for two hearings, talked to me less than 90 seconds each time, and has never looked at my son's medical documents and other evidence that I carry with me to every hearing.

January 1, 2019: I just now looked at my mail that didn't come until late yesterday evening. There is a letter from the court. It says a pre-trial management conference was scheduled for 12/18/2018 and that all witness lists and evidence were due by 12/21/2018. My attorney has none of this information and I'm being informed by mail that wasn't sent out until 12/28/2018 (stamped on the envelope).

To make matters worse, the state promised me they wouldn't involve my rapist/abuser, a man I'm greatly afraid of. They said it would be in my son's best interest not to involve him as he has a lengthy record. They lied. The letter I just opened says they sent a copy stating my name, my information, and the date for trial, to this man. He ruined my childhood and essentially scarred me for life. I never put him on my son's birth certificate. I am scared to death, angry, and hurt. It feels like a set-up.

Everyone I talk to feels bad but no one can help. The problem is legislation. I've contacted all local officials, from my local state representatives to the governor's office. However, because of elections and terms being close to an end, no one could help. Here I am. I've never been in trouble with the law in my life. Now I'm being persecuted for having a mentally ill child, and not being able to afford the $300-a-day treatment he needs. Seems there's no way to help a parent get the treatment her mentally ill child needs without charging the parent (me in this case) and labeling her as a child-abuser. The state's stripping me of my parental rights and sending me a bill for my son's expenses while he's in their care.

I have a therapist, and after he looked at all my documents and heard the story, he was in shock and felt bad. He said, "Nothing can be done." It's a Catch-22. Usually, he tries to help his patients work toward a goal, but he doesn't have a goal for me to strive for. He can only allow me to vent, which, at this point, isn't enough. God help me. I don't know what to do anymore. It feels like the state of Michigan wants me dead.

Note: Sarah cancelled her court appearance for 1/10/2019. She said, "I'm too afraid to go to trial Thursday and risk being found by my childhood abuser. My concern is his being in front of me at the trial, possibly following me home, or getting my address while at the trial. I was told by the judge's secretary they would try not to disclose my address. However, I don't put it past the courts that they would hand him a document with my mailing address on it, or say it out loud during the trial."

WHAT DO I DREAM OF NOW?

—LESLIE CARPENTER

Today I'm looking at a photo of me holding our son at my older sister's wedding. So, this photo must be from February 1992. Wow, it feels like that was so very long ago . . .

As we were watching her wedding, held in the same Presbyterian Church in Gouverneur, New York, where my husband, Scott, and I got married, I can remember imagining our son growing up and getting married as well. So many things we imagine for our children, the hopes and dreams most of us share—for them to find someone to love, to find a career that makes them fulfilled, and for health and happiness.

Well, when our son became very sick with his serious brain disorder, our dreams and hopes changed dramatically. Ever so sadly, one comes to accept that many of our dreams for our children will likely never happen. And, eventually, we process our grief, let go of those dreams, and, if we're lucky, we begin imagining new ones.

What do I dream of now for our son and many others like him? Oh my, I have so many dreams.

I dream of money being put into research to help find more effective treatments and cures for serious brain disorders.

I dream of creating wonderful psychiatric assisted living campuses with multiple levels of care from acute care hospitalization, to sub-acute units, to independent living apartments—with actual collaborative care and engagement with a team of compassionate and skilled mental health professionals and social workers and vocational rehab counselors.

I dream of establishing state-of-the-art treatment campuses that we would be proud to bring a family member with a brain disorder to for help. A place where we would be proud to work, and visit, and volunteer.

I dream of collaborative community care of all sorts, including assisted outpatient treatment teams working with civil mental health courts, so that people don't have to get so sick they end up committing a crime before that level of care can be provided.

I dream of no person with a mental illness ending up in a jail or a prison, just because they are sick and haven't been able to get medical treatment.

I dream of no person ending up homeless and untreated on our streets.

I dream of our son being able to live as independently as possible and being engaged in some activity that he enjoys—whether that be his art or volunteering or even working part-time.

I dream of our son living with as little suffering as possible, with friends, family, and a caring treatment team who are invested in his well-being.

After Scott and I are no longer living, I dream that our son will be okay when we can no longer advocate and support him.

I dream of him finally having the ability to have peace within his mind and for the voices to go away.

I dream of these things, now, because of the restoration of my ability to hope, because of my National Alliance of Mental Illness (NAMI) family and attending NAMI's amazing signature program, "Family to Family."

There's No Help in the USA

—SYLVIA CHARTERS

I will never forget the night I woke up at midnight to find my 33-year-old son crawling on the floor. As I walked toward him, he yelled, "Get down! They have guns. We're surrounded."

I realized something was very wrong with my son. I got down beside him, speaking gently. I asked him, "Who has guns?"

He said, "The FBI. The CIA."

There was no one but the two of us. He continued, "We're surrounded and in danger. They can hear through the walls."

I told him, "Stay here. I'm going for Dad."

I crawled down the hallway into my bedroom, woke my husband and told him, "Something is terribly wrong with Jason. Call 911. I think our son's had a mental breakdown."

The sheriff and ambulance arrived and pretty much confirmed what I had said to my husband. That night our lives changed forever.

My son was admitted to the hospital and we were told he would be transferred to the Phoenix County Psychiatric Hospital where he would be treated and evaluated for severe mental illness. Our hearts and minds were numb, crushed. We, as a family, became broken—just like our son. Our dreams and hopes were shattered. We didn't know this was the beginning of a horrific journey that we, as a family, would travel alone with no road map.

My son was diagnosed with Bipolar 1 (psychosis). He was hospitalized for 30 days (his longest stay). Thus began numerous hospitalizations. We watched over him 24/7. He was so different. We'd lost the son we raised and learned that he'd never be the happy-go-lucky, funny, social, person we knew. The meds kept him disoriented, sleepy, and lifeless.

We began to read, research, and ask a lot of questions. We enrolled in NAMI's Family-to-Family 12-week class. Slowly we learned the devastating truth. No one had answers. We lived one day at a time. The revolving door, cycle after cycle, merry-go-round circus began—treatment, hospitalization, overdose, under-dose, multiple meds, horrific episodes of anger, violence, running away, arrests, jail, court-ordered treatment, probation, involuntarily and voluntary hospitalizations, suicidal episodes, nine petitions. "Gravely disabled." "Seriously mentally ill." Words that held stigma, shame, and loss, brought devastation.

It became clear our son needed 24/7 care. We pleaded, searched, fought, and finally obtained transitional housing—only after Jason ran away, stopped his meds, became psychotic, and a danger to himself and others. Multiple times he was on court-ordered treatment.

I wrote letters to the governor, to President Obama, to his clinic, psychiatrists, and caseworkers, holding them account-able for my son and our family if tragedy occurred due to lack of help.

Shortly thereafter, my son was placed in transitional housing with 16-hour onsite staff responsible for ensuring that meds were taken. I visited Jason daily, made him breakfast, watched him take his meds, drove him to every doctor appointment, trusting no one (health professionals, case mangers, had all let us down).

I took early retirement and became my son's caregiver. My son started to improve. The daily routine began to work. He didn't think he was sick (anosognosia) but he began to trust us. It took three years. Jason developed diabetes, high blood pressure, and gained a lot of weight, but he continued to obey us and believed us when we told him, "We will keep you safe and off the streets. However, you must continue taking your meds."

We were making progress. Then I had to file a restraining order. Jason had pushed me out of the car and threatened me. I knew, in his psychotic state, he could kill me.

After homelessness, more hospitalizations, arrests, and court-ordered treatment, the cycle took a turn for the better. With treatment, the right meds and constant family involvement in his care, we saw improvement. We wanted Jason to live independently, however we knew he wouldn't be able to take his meds without supervision. And without his meds, he'd become psychotic and dangerous, not by his nature, but because of his illness. We learned to separate the ugliness of his illness from the son we knew and loved. We made the decision to bring him home—again. We knew that no one could love or care for him better than his family. Our family bonded together, demonstrating to him that we would not desert him. Tough love doesn't work on a broken mind.

At age 67, our retirement dreams were no longer our priority. Our son was our priority. We moved from Arizona to Florida because Jason's always loved the beach. We left the care and support we had behind. Now, we pray that Florida will help our son but, truth be told, there's no help in the USA, especially not in Florida (retirement state).

What an Effing Nightmare

—LAURIE LETHBRIDGE CHRISTMAS

My son was in a locked psych unit involuntarily because he was a danger to himself (having schizophrenia and being off meds for eight months). He was psychotic and was losing weight because he'd not been cooking and eating. He didn't understand why he was there. He kept insisting that no one had the right to hospitalize him against his will. He asked to see a mental hygiene lawyer, and when she refused to get him out of the psych unit, he punched her.

My son was arrested and removed from the psych ward and taken to jail. He was charged with misdemeanor assault and sat in jail for a month. He was on no meds while in the hospital or the jail. I wrote a letter to the judge asking that he be re-hospitalized and he was then sent to an upstate hospital, which was really a prison. He was in a section for pre-trial detainees and his rights were more restricted than they were in the county jail. He sat there for eight months before they finally took him to the local mental health court down the street, where an involuntary medication order was finally granted. All in all, he was 18 months without meds.

Then, to add insult to injury, the charges against him for punching the attorney were upped to felony assault. Why would the state charge a psychotic ill person with assault while in a locked psych ward? And why would a lawyer, who is supposed to be an advocate, push the DA to raise the charges to a felony? And why did they let him sit so long without meds?

What an effing nightmare!

My son took his meds and was stable for 10 years before all hell broke loose. When it did, I started calling everyone I could find related to his issues—doctors, lawyers, and advocacy groups. Even NAMI (no help there). I was on the phone almost daily for a year. No one would help. I have a stack five inches thick of everyone I called. Then I had to stop for a minute. I was burned out. I even started a Facebook page for parents, but to no avail. This shit started in October 2012 and was not somewhat resolved until July 2014.

I still can't get over that my son sat in a psychiatric hospital for eight months without meds. My rage is often right under the surface, and I have to take a break once in a while to keep my wits. After 2014 it was still a mess, and it got bad again in 2015 even though my son was switched to monthly shots of Abilify. He became psychotic again. The fight to get his meds changed took another year and a half.

My son is somewhat stable now, but the two 18-months psychotic breaks caused some brain damage.

My Goal Is Not Happiness but Human Understanding

—JERRI CLARK

Today, extended family of our beloved son, Calvin Clark, arrive in Vancouver, Washington, to celebrate his brief but spectacular life and to mourn with us. Earlier this week, my 23-year-old son killed himself. My family and I are going to be with our emotions this weekend, in all of their complexities. Peace and gratitude to all who have reached out with love.

Deborah Wang, a reporter for KUOW, interviewed my husband and me as we packed up Calvin's apartment in Seattle. She captured some of the complex emotions that flood us and continue to surge through our systems as we process this tremendous loss and seek a path forward. My goal is not happiness, but human understanding and compassion within the complexity of life. I'd like to explain this a little more.

Accepting that happiness is a momentary and fleeting aspect of life and not the "goal," leaves room for grief, struggle, and confusion. Those equally important experiences cannot be disregarded as bad, wrong, or something to avoid. Families impacted by mental illness can seek comfort in accepting that happiness is not the only experience worth feeling.

Please find courage to sit with whatever you are sitting with right now and see the path lit before you. What is yours to say or do? What does that action look like? How will you make it manifest?

Anne Frank: "How wonderful it is that nobody need wait a single moment before starting to improve the world."

WHAT IS
THE ANSWER?

—DAWN MACTAGGART CONNOLLY

I'm asking for prayers for my 30-year-old seriously mentally ill daughter, and I want to tell you how messed up our system is for those who desperately need help.

I've traveled down this road many times with Trisha—so many times I've lost count. For a while now, I've suspected she's not been taking her meds or has been taking illegal street drugs. She's been engaging in risky behaviors that could harm herself or others. When she talks, she makes no sense and she's unable to answer questions. Her thought processes are severely handi-capped and her delusions are many. She has an apartment with services, but she will not accept the services, follow rules, take her meds, or let the staff help her. Now she's about to be evicted.

Last night Trisha showed up at my house driving a car that wasn't hers (she has no car or license) and she had lots of cash. (She has a payee and wouldn't have access to this kind of cash.) I could clearly see how sick she was. Her 10-year-old son, whom I have raised since he was three months old, hid from his mom because of her bizarre behavior. Poor kid. She's been making threats to kidnap her boys. I knew she couldn't stay here. It's unfair to the kids and unsafe. Those boys shouldn't have to

74

spend the night in fear, as we all have many times. (Sad to say that about my own daughter, but it's the illness, not her. She has no reasoning skills and is locked up in her delusional self.)

After calling her legal guardian, it was decided the only choice I had was to dial 911. I wasn't worried or embarrassed about the cops being in my driveway or what the neighbors might think. My main purpose was to get my daughter immediate help. Plus, over the years, the police have been to my house multiple times and I know many of them. They've always been helpful, but there is only so much they can do. So they transferred her to the hospital. Within an hour, the hospital staff called to say, "We're releasing your daughter. She's fine." Now my seriously mentally ill daughter is missing. The hospital denied her critical care for the simple reason there is no critical care for the most gravely mentally ill. I could go on and on, but I'll stop here and ask for prayers that Trisha will be located, that she'll be safe, and will find help.

Things I know:

- Taking a very sick loved one to a hospital, only to have them leave with an appointment card and more meds, is not the answer.
- Putting a sick loved one in an apartment, with all new furniture and staff who pop in once a day, is not the answer.
- A doctor's 10- or 15-minute med check meeting is not the answer.
- A short, little visit with a therapist that doesn't address real issues is not the answer.
- A natural consequence is not the answer.
- A state hospital—if the state even has one—is not the answer.
- A psych unit in a hospital that houses and medicates is not the answer.

- Encouraging, positive talk from family is good, but it is not the answer.
- Posting house rules—with expectations and consequences—is not the answer.
- A list of social activities is not the answer.
- Buying new clothes and stuff is not the answer.
- Refusing to buy anything is not the answer.
- Giving money is not the answer.
- Buying cigarettes is not the answer.
- A group home with 24-hour supervision is not the answer.
- Answering what seems like 50 calls a day is not the answer.
- Family time is not the answer.
- Life-skills training is not the answer.
- A 72-hour evaluation is not the answer.
- Probation is not the answer.
- Jail is not the answer.
- Setting your children up with everything you can think of to give them a sort of quality of life while allowing them to maintain some kind of independence, is not the answer.

I'm beyond frustrated with everything. I think we're up to 40-plus facilities my daughter's been in. I'll be writing letters, again, to all my representatives here in Iowa.

Will someone please tell me, "What is the answer?"

Helping My Daughter Have a Childhood

—ELIZABETH COURTOIS

A lot of people think childhood mental illness doesn't exist. A lot of people tell me it's just normal kid stuff. It's not.

When we give birth to our children, we expect a wonderful childhood. We have hopes and dreams. We look forward to watching them learn to ride a bike, go off to their first day of school, and experience the awkwardness of having a first romantic partner, however innocent it may be. That was me in October of 2008.

It's currently August 2017 and I'm wondering if my daughter Eva will even be able to finish a full year of school—because she hasn't ever really finished one. In kindergarten, we first entered the world of psychiatric hospitalization. She made it until the last four days of kindergarten. In first grade, she was pulled out on an extended medical excuse a couple weeks before the end of school. In second grade, she was placed under a court order and pulled out of school a full month early.

Because, you see, Eva's been diagnosed with childhood-onset schizophrenia. And for whatever reason, February to June are the worst for her. Nothing stops you in your tracks faster, as a mother, than your seven-year-old with a feral, blank stare in her eyes and a Santoku knife in her hand, ready to charge. Or bar-ricading herself in your living room screaming strings of words that make zero sense. Or pounding her head into a glass window so the voices will stop. Or taking a butter knife and showing me exactly how she plans to end it all. So the voices will stop. So the chaos will stop.

My daughter's had two suspensions for intentionally trying to injure staff at school. Her teacher said, "The child disappeared out of her eyes and something else took over—a hijacked brain making it impossible to be a normal eight-year-old child."

Eva's never known a real childhood. All she knows is psych hospitals, doctors, and medications. Nevertheless, we love her—her three sisters and I. We are her warriors. We are her protectors. We take her abuse because we know she doesn't mean it. We all understand she's not a physically affectionate individual. But she shows us affection when she draws us beautiful pictures, when she decides to be more social and play Barbies with her sisters, and when she makes a paper tiara and puts it on my head and dubs me "Princess Mommy."

We never expected this. We never asked for this. But this is what life has given us. It's not easy. It's often frustrating, emotion-ally draining, and physically exhausting. But Eva's my daughter. My life's blood. And I will do what I need to do to make sure she can attempt to have a childhood.

Our Family Tragedy

—SONIA FLETCHER DINGER

My daughter, Christina, was a lovely girl, a college graduate, a good student, beautiful and smart. She was diagnosed with schizophrenia after she shot and killed her father on May 13, 2010. She had no history of arrests or violence. Drug tests were clean.

She had been having mental problems since leaving home for college, but we were unaware of the severity of her illness. She was trying so hard to be normal. Two years earlier, Christina had been committed for three days on a psychiatric hold for "mania," but we thought it was a fluke and that she had overdosed on a nicotine patch while trying to quit smoking.

After that commitment, she saw a psychiatrist for a few months who put her on Abilify, but she was not told she had schizophrenia, though she now believes that she presented ample evidence of her delusional thinking and auditory hallucinations. There are so many steps along this road to tragedy at which there was a chance for the story to take a different turn, but the stars did not align in our favor.

By 2010, Christina had graduated with a degree in Sociology from UC Santa Cruz but was unable to find a well-paying job, so she decided to go to nursing school. She moved in with her father for a few months while she completed the prerequisites. She got straight A's the first semester but started flunking tests the following semester and was having trouble sleeping. At that time she was being treated for anxiety by a psychiatrist who put her on Effexor. I believe this drug made her illness worse.

Her father and brother began calling me frequently because she stopped going to school, and was acting strangely, and they didn't know what was wrong with her. Christina was calling me daily to talk about school, talking a mile a minute. I could tell she was frantic, but she insisted the psychiatrist had told her it was just anxiety. She went back to the psychiatrist, who put her on a mood stabilizer, but it was too little too late.

The night before the shooting, I spoke with Christina and her dad and brother. We all agreed that she would move to Mount Shasta, where I live. I live in the country, where there is less stress than in the Bay Area. I wanted to help Christina, and it was hard to do that over the phone. There is a nursing school here, though not the one she hoped to attend. She wanted to drive up immediately that evening, but I convinced her it would be best to see the psychiatrist in the morning to have her medicine adjusted, and then go to school to withdraw from her classes before she drove the four hours to Mount Shasta.

Before Christina's dad went to bed that night, he asked her brother to hide the loaded gun he kept in the nightstand in his bedroom. When my son entered the room, Christina was on the phone with her boyfriend, crying, so he decided to wait. Later in the evening he grew sleepy and forgot about the gun. I don't know why my ex-husband didn't hide the gun himself.

Sometime after everyone went to bed, Christina began driving around in her car. She thought her car was "tapped" and she tried to set it on fire, because she thought voices from the FBI or CIA were coming from it. She thought someone was following her and trying to kill her. She thought she had to kill herself to prevent World War III because President Obama had spoken directly to her on TV. If only I had let her drive up earlier, or if only her dad didn't have a loaded gun, perhaps this tragedy wouldn't have happened. Everyone can think of things they should have done if they had only known.

As her psychosis raged, she drove back home and entered her dad's bedroom to get the gun and kill herself. As soon as she entered her dad's room, the voices told her to kill her dad. She says she didn't think twice. She was so ill she couldn't think straight at all. The voices commanded her.

Christina loved her dad. She told me they'd been getting along well and she was enjoying her stay with him. There was lots of news coverage and the prosecutor made up a motive. They said Christina killed her father because he was pressuring her to move out to get away from her boyfriend. The news articles didn't tell the whole story. The DA suspected me of being complicit and trying to "tip Christina off" as I frantically tried to reach her on her cell phone. I was justifiably afraid she would try to kill herself.

She was picked up by police in a park in Oakland, California, the following day, naked and covered with blood, and admitted to an acute care psychiatric hospital until she could be stabilized. She spent two weeks being "stabilized" and was immediately arrested and charged with first degree murder upon discharge. Needless to say, our family was devastated.

When I came out of shock, I hired a lawyer who did a comprehensive investigation, which found a long history of mental illness. A psychologist hired by the court agreed with the psychiatrist hired by the defense. Christina had schizophrenia. The DA lowered the charge from first to second degree murder. Christina pled guilty, avoiding a trial, and was acquitted by reason of insanity. In 2011, Christina was sentenced to Napa State Hospital for six months to life, but she awaited transfer from the jail for several months because there were no beds available.

Christina has responded well to treatment with anti-psychotic medication. (She was later diagnosed with schizoaffective disorder and bipolar disorder at Napa State Hospital.) I'm glad she didn't kill someone in the community. I would not want another family to suffer as we have. If she had, I'm sure she would be spending the rest of her life in prison. She still has a chance for a good life when she is deemed recovered. I am told she will continue to receive counseling and treatment after she is released. Fortunately, she knows that she has to take medication for the rest of her life.

Postscript: Christina was transferred to Napa State Hospital on her birthday, September 14, 2011, and released from Napa State Hospital in November of 2016, six-and-a-half years after killing her dad. She lives in a group home with other mentally ill people. She's on a conditional release program, which is like parole for serious mental illness. She's in school to become a paralegal.

I'm grateful that my daughter has a second chance for a better life. I know that so many others are spending tortured lives in prison or on the streets. If not for the fact that I had the ability to hire a lawyer to represent her, she could be spending the rest of her life in prison.

Unfortunately, there are still so many people who don't understand mental illness. My second (and current) husband is unsympathetic. He wants nothing to do with my daughter. My son, still grieving for his dad, has disowned his sister for killing him, and disowned me for coming to her aid. At this time, I'm not permitted to visit my son or my toddler granddaughters.

Our family is fractured by mental illness. I'm ashamed to say that I had little sympathy or support for my sister, who has schizophrenia as well, until the disease struck my own daughter and shocked me into realizing the truth: Schizophrenia is a brain disease that destroys a victim's ability to control their own thoughts and actions. Never in a million years would I have believed that this nightmare could happen to us, until it did.

"I Am Ashley. I Define Me."

—ASHLEY DOONAN AND CATHIE CURTIS

My daughter finally succumbed to her personal struggle with mental illness and took her life four months ago at age 26. As parents we cannot let go of our children and need to find comfort in knowing that their lives will forever matter. Here are a few of Ashley's reflections, written shortly before she passed:

I entered college severely anorexic. I wasn't really alive. But I also was so eager to learn. In high school I loved Hemingway, Steinbeck, and Sartre. I've always been a high achiever.

Frequently, I wonder what I'd be achieving if I wasn't ridden with this illness. Eventually, I overcame it. I had three research assistantships. For my MA, I received a full tuition scholarship. I was presenting at national conferences. But there were dark days. Tomorrow is the anniversary of my first sexual assault. I tried to scrub myself clean with no avail. I went to my professor's office the next day and cried. It's a feeling that I can't describe.

I moved halfway across the country for a doctoral degree. From day one, I was physically ill. I have never seen as many emergency rooms and hospital beds in the entirety of my life. I had a subdural hematoma. My brain was bleeding. I had severe withdrawals that compromised my health. I had three spontaneous seizures. But I went above and beyond to prioritize my education.

I am here because I respect and value my co-chairs and dissertation committee. I respect and value Northwestern for my acceptance. Last night, I realized that both of my professors had already submitted letters of recommendation and I almost cried. I emailed them my sentiments. These are the things that keep me going in academia when I feel like everything is falling apart. These educators are incredible to say the least.

I value education. Perhaps I'm a bit compulsive in nature. But I am ALIVE. I look at that picture of a girl on her high school graduation day that could hardly fake a smile. Sometimes, I still do that because I know that my ambitions have not exceeded my talents and I will exhibit that explicitly. I conquered something that almost killed me and lost everything I worked for.

But there are still sunflowers. And I still open my blinds to let the sun in. Yes, it's degrading. But I force a smile and remember that I have always given 100%, and that helps me sleep at night.

Growth is painful. Change is painful. But nothing is as painful as staying stuck where you do not belong. I grew amidst a time when I was losing everything I worked for. And no, it is not okay. I cried because it does things to you to always come second.

More from Ashley that I recently found on her cell phone:

You are electricity, you are synaptic connections, you are a beautiful creation of science, you are human — and some part of you wants to stay here, on this good earth where grass is still green, and the sun still makes freckles on the faces of the people who turn to her, and the moon still makes sure you are tucked in sleeping, and the cities are still full of people kissing, and you are still capable of dreaming.

I seldom use this platform anymore so it's all the more difficult to be vulnerable, but I've discovered this wonderful organization called "Project I Define Me." If you know me, you know that I'm committed to destigmatization and promoting awareness surrounding mental health.

Recently, I have overcome some of the most difficult things in my life and I'm proud to be where I am today. I want to empower and inspire others to do the same. Person-first language is so important and during this ongoing journey I've really learned how grossly misunderstood mental health is. I am more than a label or a diagnosis—I am a daughter, friend, sister, girlfriend, and Ph.D. student. I am Ashley, and I'm here to tell you that I define me.

What I've Learned About Our Broken Mental Health System

—DONNA ERICKSON

During the eight-year period of my son Ryan's many hospitalizations (14, if I'm correct), I got to see firsthand how broken our mental health system is.

After Ryan experienced his first psychotic break at nine years old, nothing prepared me for what was ahead. We had seen his deep depression, knew he had intrusive thoughts, and lived with his behavioral issues. But I wasn't aware of the extent of what his medication was doing. We had never seen a manic episode until he decided to go off his medication at age 25. What followed were eight years of pure hell for us.

We soon learned that the only way to get Ryan help was to call the police. An ambulance would arrive with a police car, and the police would begin questioning Ryan. Over time, Ryan got very good at tricking people into thinking he was okay, when he was actually very sick. Most times, Ryan would go into the ambulance, which transported him to the nearest ER. But once, he took off running down the street, until the police caught up with him. Since we were calling the police on a regular basis, they became familiar with Ryan. They knew he had a severe mental illness. Yet, we were told, "You had better do something about this"—as if we could control Ryan's mental state.

I enrolled in a NAMI Family-to-Family 12-week intensive course to learn all I could about mental illness. When I asked Ryan's caseworker about group homes, she told me, "There are no group homes." That statement was very misleading. Granted, there was no list for getting into a group home, but there were indeed group homes. They were available to those coming out of long-term stays in a state hospital.

Ryan's hospitalizations had begun in private hospitals. There were many. I soon learned that abuse is rampant in psychiatric facilities. Once stabilized, Ryan told me his stories regarding the details, and some things I saw for myself. I have since learned that all of these incidents should have been reported to the proper authorities. But we were new at this, and didn't know that at the time. The following list is what we have encountered:

1. At Faulkner Hospital in Boston, Massachusetts, Ryan was placed on one-on-one watch while psychotic. The security guard watching him refused to let Ryan use the restroom. Instead, he made Ryan urinate on the floor and clean it up afterward.

2. Psychotic patients are known to have outbursts. I'm sure it's a difficult job to work in a psych ward, but these nurses are paid well, and get to go home at the end of their shift. They, obviously, have the better deal. However, their behaviors are sometimes worse than the patients'. Instead of trying to deescalate one particular adverse situation, a nurse at Norwood Hospital said, "Ya know, Ryan, at the end of the day, I get to go home to a family who loves me. But you have nothing, and you'll never have anything in life."

3. Another time at Norwood Hospital, when Ryan was coming out of mania, he was looking very disheveled. He needed a shave and a haircut, and he hadn't showered yet. A male nurse said to Ryan, "Oh, well, don't you look like the next serial killer." Ryan was very hurt by the nurse's comment and called me on the phone. I immediately called to speak to the nurse. I told him his comments were hurtful and inappropriate. I said, "Maybe next time, you'll think and show some compassion." The nurse replied, "You're right. I tried to apologize to him, but he walked off."

   I explained that I didn't blame Ryan for walking away. I said he did that because he was so upset. I also pointed out how fortunate the nurse was that he was healthy and able to work. I let him know that my son isn't able to work because his illness is so debilitating. Ryan didn't ask for this illness, but sometimes he's made to feel as if he did—as if it's his fault.

4. The whole situation with the ER serving as a holding place is a horror show. Ryan has spent up to six days alone in a tiny room, with only a gurney, waiting for a hospital bed. I've heard that sometimes insurance companies will refuse patients if they'll get paid less by MassHealth (Medicaid). In the psychiatric ER there are no TVs, yet right down the hall, for ER patients who are not psych patients, there are TVs in every room.

   Ryan always gets worse in the ER. It's chaotic, with absolutely nothing to do there. A psychotic patient needs a calm, nurturing environment. I can't imagine living like that for even one day, never mind six. Then, if he acts up, they punish him. There's not much to take away, but I remember they took away his Bible. They also forgot to give him his medication.

5. Last summer, Ryan's doctor tweaked his medication, because Ryan was still feeling very sedated. He became manic. His doctor said this was unusual. His doctor hoped, by adding in more medication, he could stop the episode. But Ryan's illness progressed. Jeff and I were seeing the red flags. Ryan called Jeff at 2:00 a.m. saying he was lost in Bridgewater. My poor husband had to drive over to the police station, so they could figure out which street Ryan was on and bring him back to the group home. Then Jeff drove back home and had to be at work at 5:00 a.m. Not fun. But typical of what we parents go through.

WHAT ARE YOUR
FAMILY'S NUMBERS?

—DEBORAH FABOS

My son suffers from bio-neurological brain disorders. Without the right treatment and support, his medical condition prevents him from realizing that he has a serious illness. The untreated symptoms of his brain disorders control his thoughts and his actions. His untreated symptoms also control our lives.

My son has schizophrenia, anosognosia (in layman's terms, "lack of insight" or "lack of awareness" that he is ill), a history of Capgras syndrome (a psychiatric disorder in which a person holds a delusion that a friend, spouse, parent, or other close family member has been replaced by an identical imposter), a history of command hallucinations (hallucinations in the form of commands), and PTSD. So what does all this translate into? A preventable tragedy that was almost impossible to prevent.

What are our numbers? 1:6. That's our family's conservative ratio. Now, what does this ratio mean? It means that my son represents the one (1) who is suffering from his illnesses. The six (6) are the other people in our family who are directly connected to him.

Our lives have been significantly affected by his untreated or treatment-resistant medical illness. We live with constant emotional stress from the daily trauma and drama of his severe symptoms—including psychosis and crisis evaluation teams. We experience situational mental illness, like depression or PTSD, due to the hopelessness and isolation of caring for someone with a severe brain disorder when they're not being properly treated.

We've lost wages from jobs we've had to give up to care for our loved one and from having to move from one place to another due to stigma. We've missed chances of advancement at work and taken lower paying positions in order to be available to meet the needs of our son. We've faced family stress that could lead to divorce and further financial and mental decline of the entire family.

It means that my son's illness has affected more than just him. It's also impacted his school system, our local sheriff's department, the juvenile courts, and our relatives who helped provide financial aid to get him on the "fast track" to treatment. His illness dictated his and our lives—how we spent our time, our money, and our emotional resources. There was nothing left over for our needs. We were all consumed trying to save him, but we're among the lucky ones. In spite of the odds against us, our family stuck together and did what we needed to do to secure his compliance to the right treatment.

What was the cost for his intervention and treatment? Here is a start at some of our other numbers:

- Lost wages: I quit my job at DreamWorks and later at Disney on a union job that paid me $70,000 a year with full benefits. I was the only one who could care for my son.
- Mental health: I didn't have any. I lived in constant high stress of being attacked and threatened by my son along with the stress from the fear of losing him, and the stress of

not being able to find timely treatment for him. I paid not only with money, but with my mental and physical health.

- Probate Conservatorship: $6,000.
- One month in a dual-diagnosis facility before his SSI started up: $6,000.
- Qualified therapist who didn't take insurance: $160 per hour once a week.
- Equine therapy, which worked the best from all the therapies we tried: $160 per session per week.
- "Fast Track"—by-passing the waiting list for medical recipients and getting into an outpatient treatment facility that held the most promising form of treatment but didn't accept our insurance: $250 per appointment for two years until, finally, they accepted our son's MediCal.
- Blood monitor company: $150 per month. We're going on our seventh year now.
- Licensed nutritionalist: $120 per visit.
- Independent blood test for mercury and other toxins: $180.

The list goes on and on. Our son's been in therapy since second grade to work on the behavior we were trying to deal with daily. We spent and lost thousands of dollars. We have little saved for retirement, and my husband and I are 57. It was worth every penny and every sacrifice. When we look at and enjoy our son today, there's no price we can put on his life or on how close we all are now.

The problem is, why should we have to pay such a high price for medical treatment for our son? What about the families who don't have the resources we did to secure early intervention and compliance to treatment? How much worth can you give to a life?

What if my son decides to be noncompliant in the future? What would our fate be then? All this affects and still concerns my whole family. My son's illness isn't just his illness. It's a 1:6 ratio in our family. I'm not counting my brother's suicide at 15 or my mother's issues and how they impacted us.

What are your numbers? There are no statistics that include family numbers in their studies. We're the ones they don't know about or talk about. We're more invisible than the ones we advocate for. It's up to us to unify and speak out in one voice for what we need—for our rights to get appropriate treatment for our loved ones. It's their illness, but it affects us all.

I Am Livid, Shaking

—HEIDI FRANKE

I took my youngest son, Mitchell, to the hospital last night for paranoia and visual hallucinations. Upon my return home, my oldest son showed me a gun his brother purchased a week ago. No one had told me about the gun before.

I am livid, shaking. Waiting for the police to take this weapon of destruction away. The gun was not reported stolen, but it could be. The police say there are gun owners who don't write down serial numbers so, when it's taken into evidence, they can't trace the owner. The most bewildering thing to me is how much the senior police officer doesn't seem to know about Utah's gun laws. I'll call the detectives next week and ask them to pursue finding the person who sold the gun to my son. It was an illegal sale as my son has no ID.

The hospital was going to release my son this morning. When I told Mitchell he couldn't come back to live with me, he had a meltdown and the hospital realized how sick he is. Now, they're transferring him to an inpatient psych hospital that has an open bed. He has to be stabilized on meds.

The hospital crisis worker called and she "got it." She was perplexed about my son's access to a gun with his history. I also reminded her of his suicide attempt two years ago. She was calling about his health insurance. The Medicaid he has under mental health disability needed to preauthorize Mitchell's admission to the psych hospital. If my son didn't have Medicaid, he'd have a much harder time getting admitted.

I feel traumatized but can't really place the emotions anywhere. So many *what-ifs*. I'm lucky we're all still alive. My son was so psychotic last night. My husband said, "I'm glad Mitchell didn't try to shoot the aliens trying to get into his mind by shooting off bullets in the house." Mostly my son would have taken the gun to his own brain to get rid of the intrusive thoughts.

Guns are out there being sold, folks. We must have stronger restrictions. It won't be perfect but, my God, what value do you place on a child's life? Your child's life? Put your guns in caskets, not our children.

Our nation is a mess full of freaking a-hole cowboys and mental health care that is a tragedy. Innumerable parents and guardians are trying, behind the scenes, to get help for our children. Many, many of us. Yet we feel powerless to change this abysmal system with its lack of beds for treating our mentally ill. And I'm a nurse who knows the system well.

My son is a beautiful young man inside and out. He's just seriously ill with a brain disorder. I love him so much.

THIS IS
EXHAUSTING

—JULIA GILLIES

Trying to navigate the mental health system is difficult. It's a quagmire of obstacles and parents are often ignored. I've spent years trying desperately to get my two adult children the help they need, and countless hours researching everything I can on mental illness.

Now, I'm finding that I'm fighting for my daughter, Chelsea, to be taken off anti-psychotics, while I'm fighting for my son Andy to be put on anti-psychotics. HIPAA is a true hinderance. Also, lack of knowledge in the mental health community is astonishing.

For example, a friend told me to read Dr. Xavier Amador's book, *I Am Not Sick, I Don't Need Help*. Dr Amador wrote about anosognosia. Wow! I finally had a medical explanation why my son didn't think he was sick. I asked my son's doctor if he thought my son had anosognosia and he said, "No." The reality is, most mental health professionals don't know what anosognosia is.

After 11 years, numerous hospitalizations, jail, arrests, police calls, and sleepless nights worrying, "Is he dead or alive?" my son still doesn't think he is sick. I should mention he had his first psychotic break in 2008, a year after he found my eldest son, Michael, who had hung himself.

I fought hard to get Andy into the New Jersey Assisted Outpatient Program in 2014, but it fails over and over again. A simple solution would be a law that mandates people, court-ordered into the program, be picked up within a few days to get their medication.

My daughter is another story. She was sexually abused as a little girl. She was diagnosed with possible bipolar at age 16. Nevertheless, she worked hard in school and was accepted to many schools at the same time her elder brother took his life. She settled on Syracuse University to study biomedical engineering. In October 2009, I received a call that my daughter had jumped from the fourth floor of a parking garage. She survived and a psychiatrist prescribed an antipsychotic, risperidone. In 2013, Chelsea managed to graduate second in her class and received the Renee Crown Award, the school's highest award. However, I noticed she was exhibiting gait and memory issues.

In October 2017, Chelsea was admitted to the hospital with suicidal ideation and induced psychosis from being removed from risperidone too quickly. Almost two years later, she was released from the hospital with drug-induced Parkinson's disease. She has severe memory loss and right hand tremors.

This year, my daughter almost died again. When she regained consciousness, she was psychotic, and HIPAA is preventing me from being involved in her medical care. Chelsea listed Andy as her main contact, even though he's been institutionalized since March 2019.

In my opinion, research needs to catch up with the mental health community. HIPAA laws need to be reformed. Law enforcement personnel need better training. Assisted Outpatient Treatment needs legal backup. Big Pharma needs to educate prescribers about possible withdrawal and symptoms and other side effects.

I haven't mentioned the advocacy I've done with government and county mental health departments and agencies. I have a binder full of emails and documentation.

This is exhausting.

We Need
a Revolution

—JEANNE GORE

I'm a mom whose son has been hospitalized 42 times in the last 14 years. He's been beaten by seven police officers in Burlington, Vermont, homeless, missing, jailed, and on and on . . .

I'm sitting in my home on the eve of Valentine's Day thinking I should feel grateful that my son is in #ABedInstead. Instead, I am devastated. He was taken to an emergency room last Friday and then transferred to another emergency room with a locked unit for those who are suffering from a psychotic disorder, because the psychiatric facility didn't have a bed available.

I went to visit him yesterday. A nurse met me at the door and led me to his room. The room was completely stark, with white walls, a gray chair, a tray stand with some food on it, and a hospital bed where my son was lying facedown.

He didn't speak at first, so I began speaking, trying to fill the void. He looked exhausted and just plain beaten down. I wanted to hug him and tell him how much I loved him. I told him how sorry I was that he was there and tried to reassure him that he would get his meds adjusted and be home before he knew it.

He became agitated when he asked if I could take him outside to have a cigarette and I explained that I couldn't because it was against hospital rules. The nurse decided that was my cue to leave.

All the way home and ever since, all I can think about is how angry I am that we couldn't have gotten adequate treatment for my son early on to prevent this from happening to him anymore. He had insight 41 hospitalizations ago, but instead he was allowed to go through that revolving door—and out of hospitals that never kept him long enough to stabilize him.

I fought long and hard for AOT (Assisted Outpatient Treatment) laws and better commitment laws in Maine where we live, and finally we have them, though there is still tweaking to be done. My son does have AOT now, thankfully, so we no longer have to wait for him to become a danger to himself or others before we can get him to a hospital, but, after suffering 12 years without real treatment and losing too many precious brain cells, I fear he will never have insight again.

I live in a state where we also have gravely disabled and need for treatment standards, but no one uses these because there aren't enough beds. We know that CIT (Crisis Intervention Training) for police officers saves lives, but many of our officers are not trained. Police departments in Maine can't afford the training program, along with the cost of having to pay officers overtime so that each officer can take the 40-hour course.

We've expanded our forensic hospital and our mentally ill are filling up our jails. Meanwhile, our treatment providers are struggling with a state that wants to cut the pay of their psychiatric nurses by 40 percent. Does anyone else see what's wrong with this picture?

If we were able to treat people with serious mental illness, they wouldn't continue to go through revolving doors—in and out of our hospitals—and we wouldn't be arguing over the budget. We'd be saving money, and more importantly, saving lives. My son deserved so much better and every person suffering with a serious mental illness deserves so much better.

Today I read of patients being shot in hospitals, patients being sent to jail because there are no beds, Oregon talking about passing a law that would allow them to starve their mentally ill and those suffering from dementia to death.

We can't allow this to continue. I don't know when this country lost its human decency toward its most vulnerable citizens, but it surely has. I say we need a revolution and we need one now. We need to organize ourselves and protest all over this country immediately. We owe it to our children and their children to provide a country where all of our most vulnerable are treated with love, care, respect, and compassion.

Jesse and Me

—VAL GREENOAK

I'll never forget, after Jesse got his initial diagnosis of schizo-phreno-form disorder, he was sent to a special school. He was sixteen. When we were asked to meet with a social worker, we thought it would be more of the same as we had been trying to understand what was going on with him.

The social worker asked us to detail the problems we had with each other. Jesse and I looked at each other and he said, "I don't have any problems with my mother." I agreed, saying we had no problems with each other, except those that the illness caused. I am not saying that if he didn't have schizophrenia we wouldn't have had problems. It's just that any psychological problems we might have had if he was not ill just paled before the illness.

The social worker posted in the notes—which I saw after his death—that Jesse and I were both in denial. Not so. We were so close. He appreciated so much that I always reached out through his illness to reassure him. He felt I understood him. We both knew we were up against something huge.

During his lifetime we really made progress. He was better at age 24 and getting a handle on things. If we could have made it till he was in his late twenties, I could have brought him home. But no. They told me I was trying to hold him back after he went through a two-month training, and I said it was too soon to put him in a board and care facility. He was too ill, I felt, though I had no idea how completely unsupervised he would be.

My experience is that Telecare calls houses "board and care" when they offer no food (the dictionary definition of "board" is food). Because of a Telecare mistake about Jesse's SSI check, they didn't take money out of his check for feeding him. They neither fed him nor gave him money to purchase food, and he wasn't able to access free meals at the food kitchen blocks away. He was too disorganized to get there.

Telecare got lazy the week after Christmas and failed to give him his meds. They were supposedly training him to take his meds on his own and they didn't check on him for five days.

The day before he was killed, the other patients in the house told Telecare he needed to be 5150d. The staff ignored this warning, and when they discovered their mistake, a LVN tried to correct Jesse's decompensation by giving him an anti-depressant—a drug I'd told his doctor was not okay to give him. I'm a psych tech so I knew this, but had a court-appointed conservator to manage his mental health treatment, so I had no say.

From an unsupervised kitchen, Jesse picked up a sharp knife because he'd become afraid. I didn't know at that time that Telecare's crisis intervention team had been unfunded. They called the cops saying he was chasing a patient with a knife, which the patient testified Jesse wasn't doing. The cops came and gunned him down after calling him out of the bedroom where he was sequestered. They killed him less than two minutes after they got there.

I didn't live close enough and wasn't notified until too late. Watch your kids, parents, even if they are conserved. Don't ever imagine that a for-profit system will truly care for them. Trying to claim your personal problems are psychologically based is only one way the system marginalizes parents, especially when your children, adult or otherwise, are profoundly ill.

Blessings on all who are dealing with this illness and the system that's only motivated by profit. I keep you all in my heart.

I Feared He'd Be Blown to Pieces

—DEBORAH HARPER

Jared was my second son, born into our family of two boys in 1991. He was a quiet child, deeply intuitive and sensitive, musically gifted, and athletic. A boy full of life and funny faces and stories. He always made us laugh. Our Jared.

As he approached his junior year in high school, life began to take twists and turns that led us to seek help. The hope was always that help was just an appointment away. Then, as Jared became an adult at the ripe old age of 18, privacy laws separated us. I was behind an immovable glass wall, unable to reach him. HIPAA stood guard like a heartless warden of his declining mental health. The nightmare began, and evolved into multiple chapters of heartwrenching sadness, agonizing decisions, and defeating barriers.

My boy needs continuous prayers. He's been in a group home for three years. I had to make him homeless in order to make him eligible for residential support. He spent seven months in a respite bed, above an overdose crisis lock-up treatment center in the worst area of Worcester, Massachusetts, waiting for a bed in a group home.

This past year, Jared grew more depressed over his circumstances and wanted desperately to return home. He began self-medicating with alcohol. The house set up a protocol to call an ambulance if they believed he was intoxicated. The ambulance brought the police, and because Jared suffers from paranoia and schizophrenia, he didn't believe the police were real police. They grabbed him, he pulled back, and they proceeded to beat the daylights out of him. They beat him so badly he had to be taken to the hospital.

North Hallway, Position 8—A bed with a confused, hungry, and lost young man could be found in that hallway on a gurney. His illness, schizophrenia, was treated like a crime. His ride to the hospital began with a knee pressing into his neck, and tight, cold wrings that left behind purple shadows of remembrance on both wrists. He was surrounded by at least six or seven other hallway mates. They also bore the markings of a war-torn life battling the disease that we treat as dirty. I saw dirty hair, dirty clothes, and listened to dirty mouths. Whispering and cries were the audible clues they were suffering. No one was offered a drink of water. I observed avoidance. Did I detect annoyance?

Twenty long hours in that hallway waiting for the next step. This was a crisis—so many in need and so few helpers and healers. I was there for him, but no one showed up for any of the others. The lost and neglected souls of the North Hallway.

After the hospital, Jared was locked up at a Worcester police station and bail was posted. He had to appear in court to be charged with assault on police. When he arrived at court, they put him in lock-up all day. The judge heard his case at 4:30 p.m. He ruled that Jared was a danger to himself (drinking) and others (resisting police). They sent him to a Plymouth, Massachusetts, correctional facility for a mandatory 90-day rehab. This rehab required that he live in a cell, wear an orange jumpsuit, and be treated like a criminal.

My son tried calling me yesterday, and it took four minutes to set up an account to pre-pay $1 per-minute to talk to him. By the time I did that, he'd hung up. I could barely breathe.

The grief and feelings of helplessness are indescribable. The mentally ill are so drastically mistreated and misunderstood. There are no beds available in genuine rehab places because of the opioid crisis. The only places left are correctional facilities.

Distress worsens mental illness. Mental health care is a system built on failure and supported by a nation that stigmatizes mental illness. It's only recently recognized that we're still in the dark ages when it comes to treating diseases of the brain.

January 19, 2019: Jared was just released from a 40-day imprisonment at a house of correction followed by a 35-day inpatient hospitalization at a state hospital. He had a psychotic break in late October while visiting me for a few days. He believed I was part of the KKK and pulled a kitchen knife out of the knife rack. He didn't hold the knife up to me and I never saw what kind of knife he pulled. I called for help, reluctantly, because we had just had a three-year case dismissed for assault and battery on a police officer because Jared resisted them last time I called them.

The local police called in what is a called a STOP team, which I would classify as a SWAT team. Heavily armed men unloaded from vans and surrounded our house. They appointed me the negotiator and hooked me up to a speaker inside the house while a robot took photos inside the house. My small dog was inside with Jared. It was cold and raining. Every 45 minutes I had to stand three feet away from two men holding automatic weapons and one holding a shield and a taser. I was shaking like a leaf. I was luring my son into a trap. If he did anything threatening, I feared he'd be blown to pieces. Team members were in the woods, too. I could see little red lights coming from their weapons and helmets—a scene from Star Wars. The Ewoks in the woods. They evacuated my neighbors. It was insane.

After an eight-hour standoff, the police smashed a battering ram through Jared's particle-board bedroom door that didn't have a lock, destroyed his room, stepped on his guitar, and arrested him. They charged him with attempted murder among three other trumped-up charges.

I started a Go Fund Me campaign and borrowed money from my family to pay for a private attorney. The court appointed attorney was definitely not paying attention and cared very little about Jared's rights.

The local newspaper wrote a story that made my son sound like a terrorist—I believe to justify the manpower that was brought to the neighborhood. Over 25 state police cruisers, two local police departments, and an ambulance surrounded my home and lined my street. I wrote to the paper and asked to tell my side of the incident. They featured me and my story on the cover of the Sunday edition.

Jared's back at the group home. He's stable. They're working with him to keep him busy and going to therapy and AA. I saw him yesterday. He was cleaning his room, lining up his shoes, hanging up his clothes, and tolerating my visit. In the past, he wouldn't want me in his space.

This is progress. Every day is a gift. I believe in God and the power of prayer.

I Feel Incredibly Blessed

—AMY KERR

My son is twenty-one and has schizophrenia paranoid type, ADHD, and dysgraphia (inability to write coherently, as a symptom of brain disease or damage). For the first four years of onset at age 15, we went back and forth to hospitals, through med changes—so many I can't count—anosognosia (a condition in which a person with some disability seems unaware of its existence), three different psychiatrists, trouble with the law, and three different mental health organizations with "wrap around" services. Rinse and repeat, rinse and repeat.

I read Dr. Xavier Amador's book, *I Am Not Sick, I Don't Need Help,* and used the LEAP (Listen, Empathize, Agree, Partner) approach. My fiancé and I did NAMI's 12-week Family-to-Family class. I read every medical book, article or blurb on my son's brain illnesses. Slowly but surely his medication cocktail worked, he started to understand he had a serious mental illness, and the fog of anosognosia lifted.

I gave my son his meds in the morning and in the evening every day without fail. I'd stand and have a conversation with him to make sure he wasn't cheeking them. He got better and better. We moved and I thought it would trigger him, but it didn't.

The new house, with so much natural light, makes it difficult to sleep all day, My son's back to a normal sleep schedule—almost. Most days he's at peace. His new room makes it impossible for him to barricade, and he's stopped putting knives under his mattress. So I've started letting him take his own meds. He tells me he's taken them, and even told me when one of them was running out. (That's huge!)

Yesterday, I read an article from the National Institutes of Health (NIH) about some studies that are being done (NIH is not too far from my house) on schizophrenia and cognitive loss. My son's cognitive loss is absolutely awful and, at times, painful to watch. I asked him if he'd like to be part of the study and help others. He became angry, "You know how long it's taken us to find these meds that work. They'll make me go off of them and I'm not willing to go back there."

He walked away agitated, but for me it was tremendous. He acknowledged the meds work and had insight. Today, I celebrate this like he's just received a college degree. If he never gets any better than this, I couldn't be happier. Though it may sound strange, I feel incredibly blessed.

NIKKI
AND KEVIN

—NIKKI LANDIS

So this is what severe mental illness does. My husband was my dream man. He was wonderful. We had fun and laughed and traveled and made plans. And then, slowly, I lost him. It started in little bits. Barely noticeable. I thought I was imagining it. Then he convinced me I was the crazy one. Because that's what they do . . . anosognosia. It's like trying to convince someone with Alzheimer's that it's 2018. Or that they have Alzheimer's. You can't. You can't convince someone who is psychotic that they're sick.

Honestly, I thought I was losing my mind. After all, he was working, right? He could carry a gun and arrest people and do paperwork, right? But he was barely functioning. Not getting his work done. And paranoid. Crazy paranoid. He started telling everyone I was cheating. That I was staying out at the bar all night. But here's the thing—I don't go to bars and I certainly never stayed out all night. I had no idea he was spreading these things around. And his work buddies had no idea it wasn't true. Because who thinks *psychosis*, right?

Slowly he lost more of himself until he had a full and complete breakdown. It was terrifying and heartbreaking and yet hopeful. Because we had answers. And knowing the problem is half the battle, right? But it's not. Because the psychosis kept coming, harder and faster. People don't understand. They don't know what to say. They have all these ideas about mental illness from movies. Movies about mental illness are mostly crap.

You want to know what serious mental illness looks like? Go talk to homeless people because, for weeks at a time, Kevin lives in his car. He is right now. He is currently sleeping in his car. He won't shower for days—by choice. He says he just can't do it. He is completely unable to take care of our children. And you know how sometimes people with Alzheimer's hate their family members? Yeah, that too. Aimed squarely at me. I'm Satan.

I have an entire list of treatment facilities, programs, and therapies but he has to go, and he won't. He wants to live in a car. This is what nobody tells you about serious mental illnesses like schizophrenia, bipolar, and schizoaffective disorder.

Many of those homeless people you see with mental illnesses? They have families who love them. They aren't kicked out or banished from the family. They can't get treatment because they're too sick to know they're sick. Their families are members of Facebook groups that post pictures of homeless people all over the country so they can find their loved ones.

Sometimes an ill family member gets paranoid and takes a bus out of state. Sometimes the group home responsible for their care actually sends them off on a bus without telling the family. Yes, this happens much more than you would guess. Sometimes they're like Kevin and are too sick to live at home, but refuse a hotel or friend or family member. But many times they are loved and missed and looked for and prayed for.

Kevin was an inpatient twice in April alone. Kettering Hospital sent him to a Wilmington parking lot in an Uber and didn't even let me know. I requested that the social worker try to get assisted housing for him. He needs help and he won't let me help him. But they didn't even try. And don't ask about the VA. I'm not ready to talk about that situation yet.

When Kevin is relatively stable and not sick, he tells me to talk about his story. He's not ashamed and neither am I. I guess raising kids with autism gave me a thicker skin. But people need to know. Before Kevin got so sick, I didn't know. He's sick and there's nothing I can do to help him. I am putting the kids first, and I pray that some day he is in recovery and says I made the right decision. I know the old him would say I'm making the right decision. I miss that Kevin.

Schizoaffective disorder, PTSD, and OCD. That's the latest. But it doesn't really matter. All serious mental illnesses are a variation of Alzheimer's, and we don't let people with Alzheimer's live on the street and claim they have a civil right to choose it.

My heart is breaking. Our kids' hearts are breaking. Please pray for us, and if you have a family member with a brain disease/mental illness, rethink how you talk about it. I have never been ashamed of my boys with autism. Talk about it without stigma and the stigma disappears.

I know I have so much to be thankful for. My family's been blessed beyond measure in so many ways. I go day-to-day relatively happy. And then it will hit again and I just want to cry. I don't always get to because there's a little face that needs to be kissed or a little behind that needs to be wiped and I don't want them to see me so sad. But sometimes I just need to cry.

I am such a fighter and that's not always a good thing. I've accomplished so many things that were supposedly impossible, and because that's my nature it makes this harder. I seem to always be looking for ways to figure everything out so we can have the life I envisioned, even when it's not something I should be fighting for anymore.

Has anyone else beat this? How do you let go of dreams without hating the person with serious mental illness who has stopped those dreams? Or without hating the system that makes it so hard to get better and live life again?

EVERYONE NEEDS HOPE

—MARTHA

I wrote "Everyone Needs Hope" in 2015 when I had the opportunity to go on a five-day vacation. As you know, vacations are rare to go on when you are a full-time caregiver to a loved one with a serious mental illness (or neurological brain disorder). For the first time in 15 years, I had asked two close family members to help with my son while I was away.

I was anxious about being away and, yet, I tried to enjoy myself. By the third day of my trip, one of the family members who was helping my son sent me an email with the subject line, "Good Read." When I opened the email, there was a link entitled "Enabling-Enabler-Resources." I was completely crushed. What a memorable trip for all the wrong reasons.

When I got home, I called my brother-in-law, who is a retired career Air Force veteran and lives a long distance from us. He'd been stationed in Afghanistan, at one point, during the Afghanistan war. I knew he'd suffered from mental illness, temporarily, and I wanted to share my pain with him. He empathized with me and said, "I have only a glimmer of understanding of what individuals with chronic serious mental illness experience every day. I suggest you try being placed in a dark well for three straight days, 500 feet down, with a hood over your head, to get a sense of what I experienced during my depressive episode. That might give you some understanding of what SMI folks live with on a day-to-day basis. We all, as human beings, need hope. Mental illness causes us to lose hope. We all need a north star, that unconditional love, that thing to hang onto. Martha, don't ever forget, you are that north star for Derrick."

My brother-in-law's words and complete understanding prompted me to write this piece and I've carried it quietly with me ever since. I know my family dynamics and that this kind of understanding will take time.

EVERYONE NEEDS HOPE

We all, as human beings, need hope. Mental illness causes us to lose hope. We all need a North Star, a compass, a twinkle of belief, unconditional love, a thing to hang onto, a reason to take our medicine.

I have been in the trenches with my son, Derrick, for 15 years now. You have not been by my side, not seen what I have seen, not had to make the decisions I have had to make. Not just for a day or two or three but every day. Therefore, you have no right to lecture or criticize me on my decisions or actions because all it does is hurt me. It doesn't help me and I can't accept that. I need to stay focused on the positive. I need to replenish my energy. I know all of the love and effort I've put forth. That is the truth of the situation and I know that Derrick knows it, too. I know I've made progress over the years. It may have only been an inch at a time, but it's progress. I can't begin to imagine where my son would be today without me. Therefore, I know we've made progress.

Have I done everything perfectly throughout the years? Absolutely not. I've done the best I know how with the information and resources I've had available to me at a given time.

Do I have regrets? Sure I do. Mental illness is complicated. I'm doing the very best I can with what Derrick's illness allows. His decisions are not always the ones I would like for him to make, but I have to try and accept them.

One of Derrick's doctors once told me, in reference to his mental illness, that I needed to conserve my energy because this is not a short run but the start of a marathon.

That's a daunting thought—the start of a marathon of caregiving.

If knowing what I know today, along with the uncertainty of what will come tomorrow, would I still have made the commitment to begin this race? Yes. Derrick didn't choose his mental illness—he was only 16 years of age with an amazing future ahead of him—just as no one chooses cancer, diabetes, or Alzheimer's. The race we start when we begin caring for those we love is challenging and hard regardless of the disease, and we never know what we will learn along the way or when we will cross the finish line. I know I wouldn't be the person I am today if it weren't for the many moments I've shared with my son, and I'm forever grateful to him for that.

Early on in his illness, Derrick would occasionally look at me in a wise and patient kind of way and say, "Maybe someday you'll understand," and say no more. Those words have stuck with me and, as the years have passed, I've realized so much, received more to appreciate, and have never forgotten that everyone needs hope.

A Mother's Fight

—CAROLE MCAFEE

To: Psychiatric Security Review Board, Oregon State Hospital, and Oregon Health Authority:

Re: My son

Date: July 10, 2017

Please realize (as I have said for many years, and continue to advocate for) the least restrictive environment, where my son will not be "a danger to himself," is a structured group home setting.

In that structured living model, he is supported by staff monitoring, medication management, money management, household responsibilities, human interactions, healthy social and outdoor activities, regularly scheduled appointments, and appropriate mental health treatment. He does have a problem going to groups. He thinks more one-on-one talk therapy would help him. (I agree.)

It is unrealistic to expect him to provide these things for himself: to be safe, to be functional, to be financially responsible, to choose appropriate social interactions, or to be medically healthy in an "independent living" situation. He has done well during his time at Oregon State Hospital (OHS) in the Cottages, and when he moved into the structured group home in Bend. Then, because his time was coming to an end under the Psychiatric Security Review Board (PSRB), he was moved into an "independent living" setting; his own apartment in the community. He had minimal support or interaction. As I warned anyone who would listen, and as his history shows, he began to unravel. He went missing for an excruciatingly long week.

No one who works with him now has ever seen him in a psychotic state, or gut shot by a gang member while he was living on the streets, or near death from exercising his "civil right" of living a dangerous street life "in the community."

This time, when he left his apartment, he made it from Bend to Corvallis by bus and on foot. He had blisters on his feet, he (barely) slept on park benches, he quit taking his medication, he drank alcohol, and he had no support. Thank God he turned himself in to the Corvallis police, before being arrested, harmed, or worse. They brought him back to OSH, thanks to a missing person bulletin that had been issued.

He is beginning to recover. Nevertheless, he is not an appropriate candidate for "independent living." He ran away, and he will do it again. Why flush the last five years (of your work and his work for him to become stabilized) down the toilet? As soon as the PSRB incentives are removed, he'll be at the mission or on the streets—in imminent danger.

What about civil commitment? He has even advanced that option himself, during some of his more insightful and self-reflective conversations. He can say the words the court wants to hear to move him along through (and temporarily out of) the system. However, that will not save him from himself or from the streets or from being left in an untreated, dangerous, or in a psychotic state.

He's too old and too ill to survive on the streets and to keep having to start over. Right now, that is still preventable. He is a person with disabilities and several life threatening illnesses. He deserves medical treatment, just like a cancer patient deserves medical treatment. He deserves the treatment and support needed to reach his full potential. He is a kind, smart, creative person who functions well with support. Without that support, the costs to him, personally and to society in general, are immeasurable.

Sincerely, Carole M

8/30/18: My son is in a structured group home and is in the ACT program. He has a team of people who work with him—counselors, doctors, peers—and stable housing. This has made all the difference in the world for him. He isn't being left to fend for himself. He chooses to do things like short hikes, swimming, and community outings. He usually has a good attitude and is med compliant. He struggles with side effects and diabetes. He has an eye infection which could lead to blindness if he doesn't use steroid eye drops. Recently, he had a bike accident which required surgery on his wrist/hand and a cast. He also fractured his elbow. So he has to go from being somewhat active to resting and healing.

"We Don't
Help People Here."

—ANGELA MCCANDLESS

My son Dillon McCandless is 29-years old. He was diagnosed with paranoid schizophrenia in 2014 after we had him involuntarily committed to the state hospital here in Idaho. When he was released, we thought that medication was all that he needed.

Dillon saw a psychiatrist twice after his release. He did well for about a year and a half and he thought he was cured and went off the medication. It wasn't long and his symptoms returned. We got him back on the medication but it never really worked well the second time around, and he began to use drugs and alcohol to cope. This made everything worse.

We tried to get him back into the hospital but we were unsuccessful in our attempts. We went to the prosecutor over mental health and he said, "If he isn't a danger to himself or others, it won't happen." We tried the state hospital and our local mental health office.

Five weeks later, while having a psychotic episode, our son robbed a casino that was on the Indian reservation, making this a federal crime. We told his lawyer of his illness and asked him if there was something he could do to get him some help. He said, "We don't help people here."

We didn't like his answer so we met with the federal prosecutor and Dillon's lawyer together. Instead of getting him help,
they sent him to San Diego for a competency evaluation to see
if he was competent to stand trial.

Dillon was gone almost three months and, when he returned,
he had lost 45 pounds. He was moved six times before making
his way back to Idaho. The report stated he was competent to
stand trial. At his competency hearing, the judge could see he
was having problems. The judge ordered the prosecutor and our
son's attorney to get a psychiatrist to see him on a regular basis
and adjust his medications if needed. This never happened. (We
have the audio recording of this order.) Dillon was in a county
jail here in Idaho (a federal hold jail).

The physician assistant prescribing didn't know what she
was doing. She let Dillon prescribe his own medications but
didn't know how to dose him. At times, the jail didn't medicate
him at all and let him go cold turkey. He began to self-destruct
and broke his foot. At the time of his change of plea hearing,
he was unmedicated and walking on a broken foot. Later, he
broke his hand.

His lawyer did nothing for him. He told us the reason no
psychiatrist saw our son was because the US marshal refused
to pay for one, but we found out the request wasn't made. The
prosecutor who was ordered to get the psychiatrist said, "Well,
you don't get Cadillac care in jail."

Our son got worse and punched a guard, and the guard broke
Dillon's shoulder. Inmates called us and told us they knew Dillon
was going downhill. They were requesting medications for him.
He wasn't able to even get ibuprofen. We called his lawyer, county
mental health, the jail, and the judge. Dillon's cellmate told us
that Dillon was building a fort under his bed and hiding in it.
Even the guards weren't helping him. It took the jail 60 days to

X-ray Dillon's broken foot, several weeks to X-ray his hand, and a week to X-ray his shoulder.

After the altercation with the guard, Dillon was tased and put in isolation, where he tried to kill himself. He was taken by ambulance to the local hospital to have his wrists glued shut. After the suicide attempt, the county tried to get him into the state hospital. We made a personal visit to the county prosecutor. He was getting paperwork filled out, but the US marshal refused to let him go to a hospital. The prosecutor was shocked by this.

Instead of getting him help, the authorities moved Dillon to another county jail and moved up his sentencing date. Inaccurate information about medication compliance was used against him in the pre-sentencing report. He was given nine years—two years for the robbery and seven years for use of a firearm. Pretty harsh for a first offense.

Dillon was moved from Idaho to Victorville, California. While he was there, a doctor said, "I have no idea why he was sent here. He is too sick for us to take care of him." She moved him to the Federal Medical Center in Rochester, Minnesota. We were hoping that they would help him but nothing happened. Instead, he was in the SHU (the hole) for most of four months.

Dillon was refusing to take medication. He was given a shot of thorazine when he first arrived and he hated it. They wouldn't give him the anti-anxiety medication he wanted so he refused anti-psychotics. To ensure he didn't cause any problems unmedicated, they put him in the hole. They said, "We can't help him if he won't take medication."

In the federal system, they don't have to medicate you if you choose not to be medicated. I believe it's the same for the state.

Last month, Dillon was moved to Sheridan, Oregon. We saw him two weeks ago, and he looks terrible. He's very thin and still unmedicated. Our visit didn't go well because he struggled to answer our questions. He said "what" all the time.

None of Dillon's injuries have been fixed. They've healed incorrectly and cause him pain. He's declining. The federal system is a nightmare for the mentally ill. They were right when they said, "We don't help people here."

I just wanted to tell my son's story. We all need to speak up or things won't change. I know this is a long read and I've left out so much. We're still trying to get Dillon the help he needs. We have a lawyer who is trying to make sure he is getting care in Oregon, but he can't get Dillon's medical records, and we have guardianship. They say, "Dillon has to sign for them." We keep reminding him, but his memory is poor. Dillon recently had his commissary privileges taken away. He missed a roll call and pushed a wrong button. He can't think straight without medication. The mentally ill are usually in trouble.

A few days ago, KPVI had an article about Lance Quick. He lost his life after six days in prison. He went without food, water, and his medication. How incredibly sad.

There's nothing criminal about being diagnosed with a mental illness, but it's criminal how we treat individuals with mental illness. Our system is broken. We must get involved in advocating for change for our mentally ill.

WHAT WOULD
YOU DO?

—SHERRI MCGIMSEY

Tomorrow, I have to go into a team meeting to discuss my son Matthew who suffers from schizophrenia. They want me to sign papers giving permission for them to start looking for a new placement for him. For my son and his beautiful mind. He has (for how many days?) been housed in a mental hospital ward, not the ideal place for your son to live, but it's the only place he's been stable and safe for the past year.

After fourteen years of watching him suffer through depression, delusions, and overwhelming fear, ("Having a rough time"— that's what he would call the bad days) how does a parent do this? Sign their sick child away?

If you've never seen a young adult decompensate from schizophrenia, it's like watching your loved one being tortured by his mind. You stand by helpless. Nothing you can do but love him enough to fight him to get the help he needs. I'm not sure if I'm brave enough to let him go after 53 odd hospitals stays, and five times tracking him down when he gets paranoid and does a walk-about. Will all the progress he's made, all the stability he's gained, be lost?

The only place they can find for him to live is far away. Too far for weekly visits, too far for passes on Saturday or Sunday afternoons, too far to cherish the few family moments this illness allows us. Moments others take for granted—to sit and relax, to walk the dogs, to just be with family.

Yesterday was the best he's been in years. Finding a comfortable, safe, and caring place for him to live shouldn't be so difficult. But it doesn't exist—not for our children who suffer from serious mental illness.

So I sit here shaking and wondering if will we survive another calculated risk. Another shift that could send Matthew back into the dark of his illness. He fights the horrible betrayal of his mind, and I fight a system that is broken, and a world that really doesn't understand the failure to help those who suffer with serious mental illness unless it happens to one of their own.

I'm going to let this rest for now and enjoy the remainder of my day with our other son and his family. But tell me, what would you do if you had to walk into a meeting tomorrow and sign your sick child away?

Would this broken system break your heart, too?

Too Many Families Live This Pain

—JACQUE COWGER MCKINNEY

I have struggled with this post, but my husband, Steve, and I discussed it last night and decided we want to help educate, to the best of our ability, and to help make sense of some of the madness that surrounds us.

For a while, we knew that, in Illinois, a person has the right for a jury to determine their continued treatment in an inpatient psychiatric setting. We faced a six-person jury with an alternate to determine continued treatment for our child. We worried and dreaded the situation for weeks. How could six people, who had no experience or comprehension of this illness, determine our loved one's care? It seemed to me that a qualified physician should make that determination.

Well, yesterday, we arrived at the courtroom at 9:30 a.m. and left around 5:30 p.m. The decision was for continued treatment. I admit, after being sequestered ourselves for five-and-a-half hours, we were frustrated and angry. But, after all was said and done, we realized that the worldview of seven more individuals was changed forever. They were educated on the illness as well as the insufficiency of services in our state. One juror looked at us and said, "My heart breaks for you."

I share this to say that, sometimes, we must be vulnerable and transparent for others to comprehend the nature of the beast we deal with, and for changes to be made. We're not alone. Too many families live this pain. Please pray for change in our country for the care of some of our most vulnerable.

We Received the Worst Call of Our Lives

—RHONDA METH

This is the story of the loss of our beautiful Monica, age 26. She was a great artist and jewelry designer. She was generous, loving, and caring. She passed away at the room and board that was her residence. Unfortunately, she suffered from ulcerative colitis, diagnosed at age 11. She also had depression issues and high anxiety. Monica spent way too many days, weeks, and months in and out of hospitals for physical and mental health issues.

Monica was living in an unlicensed room and board in Elk Grove, California. This room and board was supposed to be one of the better homes, according to Heritage Oaks in Sacramento. Heritage Oaks had screened the person running it and the home. For the first four or five months, the man running the home was around. Monica was stable and well balanced from her medications. The manager prepared meals for the six people living in the home. He supervised issues that came up among the residents.

Then he decided he needed more income and took a job doing construction work. He'd make breakfast for everyone and go to work early in the morning. He instructed our daughter to make lunch for all of the people living in the home. Monica worried about the other people and became anxious if she wasn't around to make the lunches. This was not her responsibility. She didn't get paid to do this. She got some extra kitchen privileges. My point is, six people with mental health issues were left on their own all day long. Monica said sometimes they wouldn't have dinner until 9:00 p.m.

The day before Monica passed away, I talked to her on the phone and she seemed to be doing okay. She was getting over a bad cold but was less stuffed up. She may have mixed up or taken too much of her prescription medications. We haven't received the toxicology report yet. I think the manager may have checked on her once during the night since her roommate was worried about her. He left for work at 6:30 a.m. When her roommate couldn't wake Monica up at 9:30 a.m., she called him and he told her to call 911. The paramedics arrived at 10:00 a.m. They worked on our daughter for an hour, but couldn't get her to breathe again. My husband and I received a call from the police department that afternoon. The worst call of our lives.

This man shouldn't be running a room and board but, after talking to APS (Adult Protective Services), I've learned there is very little accountability and few regulations these room and boards need to follow. Many of them are just collecting rent.

Have You Seen My Son?

—KELLI NIDEY

February 19, 2019

I don't usually talk about this. My eldest son, Mitch, has battled bipolar disorder for a long time, and has suffered from a head injury. He's overcome addiction and the extremes of mania with medication and religious devotion, but a few months ago he went off his medication.

Today, after the best week he's had in many years—painting a beautiful picture for me, hanging out with old friends, cleaning the house, doing a little volunteer work in the community, and walking the dog—Mitch packed his bag and left while I was in another room.

He messaged that he's headed to California because, "God wants me to save the lost there." He's taken off before and gone as far as Colorado, where he was lost in a snowstorm and rescued by a good samaritan. He went to California with a homeless veteran during a very bad time in his life. He's always survived, but I'm terrified. Every time he leaves like this, I'll get the worst kind of call or never hear from him again.

I don't know why I'm sharing now. I've been down this road so many times. I guess I'm tired. And I know there are other people struggling with PTSD or the neurological disorders that we label mental illness. I'm also hoping, if anyone sees him, they'll help him get home.

I've rented him a hotel room in Carlyle, Illinois. I feel like I am enabling him, but right now, I don't want him to freeze to death.

February 22, 2019

Mitch is hitchhiking and stayed at a hotel in St Charles, Illinois, last night—the Sleepy Inn near highway 370. He was leaving there this morning to go further west. The night before, he stayed outside and I had the police check on him. He stopped at a hospital there for back pain but he didn't stay. At the time the police talked to him, he was dressed warmly, cooperative, and spoke lucidly. They didn't feel like they had enough to force him into the hospital. The local hospital wouldn't help because he'd crossed state lines.

People helped him this evening, and he's now in Troy, Missouri. Someone fed him and bought him socks and foot medication. I rented a room for him in Troy so I can sleep tonight. I feel like I'm on a roller coaster. Mostly, I'm trying to keep track of where he is, and praying he stays warm.

My other son is away at college with his girlfriend, so he's been able to separate from the drama. I started a demanding job a few months ago. Thank God I have it or this would be even more stressful, financially.

A friend shared that her son is traveling the country in a bus he bought, and that he lived on the streets one winter. I had no idea her son was sick. We all hide and isolate.

February 25, 2019

This past weekend in Troy, Missouri, Mitch said, "I still plan to travel west."

He's walking.

TERESA AND DANNY

—TERESA PASQUINI

Danny was transferred back to Napa County Jail last Friday. Atascadero State Hospital has again deemed that he is competent to stand trial for charges that first occurred while a patient at Napa State Hospital beginning in August 2012—four years ago.

He was transferred without so much as a phone call from the hospital. The only reason we knew was because we didn't get our nightly call from him Friday night. He called us every day, twice a day, while at Atascadero, once in the a.m. and once in the p.m. We could set our clocks on Danny's calls. He never missed one. I told my husband around 7:30 p.m. on Friday night that he must have been transferred that day since he hadn't called us. It would have been considerate to have received a phone call from someone saying that our disabled son was being transported six hours across the state. It took 24 hours to know he made it safely.

The Napa County Jail has been really good to Danny and we have no complaints about his care, but we hate it when he is incarcerated. We know that he is isolated, secluded. We know he takes his medications as prescribed but we know that he gets scared and sicker. We never know when he will call and we are no longer able to visit him in person due to new rules at the

135

jail. No more touching through glass, which was bittersweet, yet more human than a computer screen.

Now we only have phone calls, video sessions, and glances in court. The video sessions have their advantages, and we are grateful for the convenience. I quickly made a video appointment yesterday for 4:00 p.m. today. I spent two hours yesterday fixing my computer to make sure the session would work. I got the green light and told Danny this morning, when he called, that we would be visiting him by video today at 4:00 p.m. and we would introduce him to the new kittens, Cali and Lucca. He was so excited and happy.

Then I received this: VISITATION SESSION CANCELLED

No reason given, just a polite email from the company that sucks incarcerated families dry with excessive phone charges. Families are the "F" word in mental health, jail, and prison systems. Families are rarely considered when it comes to adult children with serious mental illnesses no matter where they are placed. We are shunned, along with our disabled children. It is wrong. It hurts. It is unacceptable.

I am the proud mom of an adult son with serious mental illness who will *not* be forgotten in discussions about rules, guidelines, laws, and policies that affect my family. I am tired of being politely shunned and tolerated. I am tired of having no rights and tired of my son having no rights. I am tired of my son being tortured, slowly and cruelly, while everyone chit chats about wellness and recovery.

I am no longer a "recovering angry mom." I am angry and I will drive change that matters for families like mine. It is beyond time to get real and shatter the status quo. We have waited long enough.

Zac, My Darling Son
& Let's Talk About Real Issues

—LAURA POGLIANO

He was the little boy who wouldn't eat until you had lunch also.

He kissed every animal and crustacean and reptile he ever saw.

He bounced on my bed and sang in his baby lisp, "When I gwow up, I'm having wots of babies, cuz I wike them!"

He swung on our swing butt naked, singing, "It's Good To Be King,"

He loved God, and at five announced, happily, that one day he'd see his real Father, and he couldn't wait. He'd be "where everything was beautiful and there was never any pain."

He got his own feelings hurt when his puppy got scolded and when a classmate with disabilities was chosen last.

He cried so hard the first day of kindergarten, because there was too much to remember and he "forgot to make a friend."

He purposely partnered on school projects with the kid with no partner.

He refused to do homework for a teacher who made racial remarks toward the Mexicans in their class.

He told me in second grade he'd thought of a way to never have to go to college and leave me.

At nine, his goal was to marry a best friend, a girl who wasn't concerned with fashion. He thought, practically, that picking one out sooner, rather than later, was a good idea.

At 10, he went to the store and bought shoes for his friend for Easter who he thought was wearing "girl shoes."

He defended his rescue dog Butters' destruction of most of our shoes and half the house with, "You people don't understand. He's just upset cuz he got left."

At 11, he told me he might have bad news for me. Boys couldn't date their mothers, he'd discovered, so our Friday night movies had to stop.

I will never get over what happened to this child, the torment he endured, and the beautiful life he was cheated out of. He reminds me of the Cummings poem, "i sing of Olaf glad and big," especially the last line—"he was more brave than me: more blond than you."

SO, LET'S TALK ABOUT REAL ISSUES.

Stigma exists, but it's not what keeps people from care. In many cases, a person with a severe mental illness has anosognosia (the inability to recognize illness). When a person has psychosis, he isn't really too worried about stigma.

If you eradicated stigma tomorrow, literally erased it from every mind and heart in the universe, you'd still have the following:

- A broken mental health care system run by police.
- HIPAA handcuffs.
- A billion dollars a year in funding going to Kittenology and situational mental health issues instead of help for the most severely affected and evidenced-based treatments.

- Rampant homelessness and unjust incarcerations.
- Ridiculously unprepared mental health care workers, with useless psychology degrees, treating your child for a drastic medical illness.
- Quackery and charlatans.
- Legal discrimination in medical parity.
- Enormous costs for treatment, lack of insurance coverage, and pencil pushers determining length of stay and medicinal options.
- Peer recovery usurping medicine.
- A shortage of 100,000 psychiatric beds in this country alone.
- A desperate shortage of qualified psychiatrists, especially in rural areas.
- Patients who won't stick to medical regimens and act out.
- Right to Be Sick Laws and no assisted outpatient treatment programs.
- An almost complete lack, except in certain big institutions, of comprehensive, wraparound programming to rehab the patient.
- Big Pharma promoting bad drugs.
- No standardized treatment plans for recovery.
- No affordable housing and no employment opportunities.
- Anti-psychiatry whippets and naysayers.
- All the heartbreak and decimation a severe brain illness causes to the patient and family.

You just wouldn't have stigma.

Rewind
and Erase

—LINDA RIPPEE PRIVATTE

& Beyond My Understanding of
What Being Human Means

—CJ HANSON

Linda:

Today, I went and found my brother, Mark. He was lying on the sidewalk at a busy entrance to a shopping center. Cars were whizzing by. Another man was sitting there with him, and as I approached them, I could see that Mark was giving him money and asking him to count it. I was immediately suspicious. I asked my daughter to remain in the car.

I walked up quickly and called Mark's name, as I always holler his name before approaching him so not to startle him. I waited until he recognized my voice before I began conversation. Mark pulled another dollar bill from his pocket and asked me what denomination it was. I was concerned that maybe he was buying street drugs. No, that wasn't it. Here sat another homeless person who had talked my blind brother into giving him all his money to buy a gold pocket watch. He laid out $14, which was all that he had. Unless that watch could verbally tell time, what on earth would a blind, gravely disabled man need with a pocket watch?

Good thing I had brought him food, water, and clothing. Mark was shirtless, but had a very heavy coat on. Today, the temperature is supposed to reach 98 degrees. I begged him to take off the coat. He refused, saying the coat would be stolen. He was extremely sunburned already. The wounds on his face and around his empty eye sockets were still badly infected from two different beatings several weeks earlier, when he was robbed. Today, all he had with him was a small blanket. His clothing was disintegrating, as he wore the same pair of pants all through the winter and spring. He didn't have a cane to guide him. (He has had 11 different canes this past year.)

I sat down next to Mark, and within seconds, it was obvious that he was delusional. He grabbed my hands and slapped them down, hard, on his leg that has a metal rod from crotch to ankle. He held both my hands down with his hands. His hands looked like leather and were cracked and bleeding. Regardless, he continued to hold my hands tightly. His entire body was trembling. He said, "We have to go back and erase each year that has passed since June 21, 1987 (the date of his motorcycle accident)." Rewind and erase.

I was shocked that he still knew that date. Yes, it had been Father's Day, but he still remembered the actual date. He proceeded to say each year backward to 1987. With each year, he said, "Rewind and erase." He shook, violently, until he reached 1987. Then he grabbed and hugged me and said, "Now, don't you feel better?"

I told him, "Yes, and I hope you do too." He began to argue with the voices in his head, screaming that the police were implanting and growing people inside of people and controlling them. I tried to calm him and get him to eat the food I had brought him. He would take a bite, chew tiny bites, and then spit it out.

141

He brought up my twin. Mark doesn't always comprehend what I tell him, but I continue to tell him the truth. CJ, my twin sister, had gotten bad news about a medical diagnosis. I shared her condition with him. He began yelling at the voices he hears and blaming those voices for all the pain and suffering of those he loves. The intent of his body language was to beat himself up. I hugged him, and once again reminded him that I love him, as I do on every visit. He didn't want to let go and held on tight for a while. As I was saying goodby, he began crying. He said, "Someone disconnected me from my mother. They're cutting out pieces of me."

I slowly walked away, feeling sick to my stomach. If only I could rewind and erase all the horrible memories, delusions, pain, and suffering he's had for the last three decades. Yes, Mark, I would feel better.

Every letter/email I've sent out has also been sent to the County Board of Supervisors. I've sent out over 1200 emails and my twin, CJ, has sent as many. Each time, we copy agencies and politicians. We've saturated them. We've sent thousands of private messages all over the state, and made thousands of posts and comments in over 100 social media groups all over California. CJ authored the petition for AB1971* and we collected 56,000 signatures that went to the full assembly and senate. We've made 30 speeches speaking at public meetings. We've testified twice at the Capitol in support of AB1971. I've gone to the Capitol and told my brother's story to support several other bills. There have been 12 news articles and TV interviews. Mark's story has been published in three national blogs and used at medical conferences. We've friended, and are in contact with, several well-known national mental health advocates—Ron Powers, Teresa Pasquini, Leslie Carpenter, Dede Ranahan, and DJ Jaffe to name a few.

142

The Board of Supervisors are ground zero. They are aware of all that we've done. They stay silent and do not converse with our family. The next project we are working on is a documentary. I have many, many videos of my visits on the streets with Mark. We will make the videos available to politicians and to the public. They are undeniable. When they are shown, Solano County should hang its head in shame.

Note: Solano County has declared Mark to be competent.

AB1971. This bill would, until January 1, 2024, expand the definition of "gravely disabled" for these purposes, as implemented in the County of Los Angeles, to also include a condition in which a person, as a result of a mental health disorder, is unable to provide for his or her basic personal needs for medical treatment, if the failure to receive medical treatment, as defined, results in a deteriorating physical condition that a medical professional, in his or her best medical judgment, attests in writing, will more likely than not, lead to death within six months, as specified.

Beyond My Understanding

CJ:

To my twin sister Linda Rippee,

I could barely read through your post without tears flowing down my face like a stream from a mountain top. A stream that never ends. I didn't think I had this many tears left. I feel so helpless, with my own illnesses, that I am unable to help with a physical presence. The responsibility and the experience of actually interacting with Mark have fallen on your shoulders.

Is there such a thing as survivor's guilt without having actually lost someone? I can't describe the pain I feel any other way, so I'm at a loss. I'm at a loss at the pain and suffering Mark endures every day on the streets, knowing that we have no legal right to force him to live with the few of us left, nor is it even possible. Knowing that we have fought for 32 years trying to help him and make his life better, and knowing that he blames us for allowing him to live as the doctors didn't believe that he would. Knowing that the laws in this county, state, and nation are against families of loved ones who suffer from traumatic brain injury and serious mental illness. Knowing that, no matter how hard we've fought every day to change minds, hearts, rules, and laws, so far we have failed. We have failed.

I have such a hard time believing that we've failed, but we have. It matters not that we have fought every day. Every single day for 32 years. Yes, for a while he was able to live a somewhat normal life until the mental illness set in. The doctors said it would happen eventually, but what has happened to him since? The apathy of people with the power to change policies, rules, and laws is a clear indication that, not only have our efforts failed, but the lawmakers have failed.

How many potential bills have failed over and over as the lawmakers insist there is more legislation now for the seriously mentally ill than ever before. That may be true, but they keep failing. Failing the sufferers. Failing the families. Failing society. No human being should have to live without options like our brother. I am having difficulty understanding anything anymore about this travesty.

Facing my own mortality only makes me feel more like a failure. I still have in my mind that 12-year-old boy who tracked me down at a friend's house after I had moved away from home at 18, and clung to me, begging me to move back home. I still have in my mind seeing Mark that day of the accident, barbecuing at Mom and Dad's house and telling us how he wasn't going to keep that motorcycle but was putting it up for sale. I still have in my mind that he was on his way to my home, in Fairfield, that night to see me when the accident happened.

Did I fail him, Linda? Did I fail him by making the decision to let the doctors try to save him? Was I wrong to want him to live? I thought I was making the right choices while I actually had power of attorney back then. I'm not so sure, now.

What are we to do? Lawmakers and officials have tired of our continued efforts and have turned their own blind eyes away from the situation. No one who has any power to give families back their rights, or to change the laws preventing us from helping him, cares. Not really. I have no faith in lawmakers' motivations anymore. Not one has proven that they care enough about the families of the seriously mentally ill to truly push through what needs to be done to make a real difference.

I can't stop crying—for Mark, and how he lives and suffers; for you, being the last one in our family to be able to go out and find him; for myself, for being so helpless in my own infirm condition and disability; for Mom, who will leave this earth knowing her youngest child will most likely die on the streets; for all the ignorant and uninformed people who find such joy in blaming our family; for those in the community who do care and have tried to help Mark and us for so long; for our society; for this very world.

My despair and tears are beyond my ability to explain anymore. Beyond my understanding of what being human means.

Looking for Joy

—DEDE RANAHAN

& Tony's Finger

—PATRICK RANAHAN

I've been in Canada for twelve days. I departed from home on August 25, the day before what would have been my son's forty-eighth birthday. Since Pat died in a psych ward two years ago, it's been difficult to maintain my equilibrium. In Canada, I wanted to be in nature. I hoped to find some solace, some joy, some connection to my deceased son. I seem to "see" him outside—in sunsets, in moonlight, in trees and flowers. In the wind.

I miss Pat. I'm still grieving. The part that concerns me about myself, however, is something else. My anger. Why did my son live a life of such hope and despair? Why did he die when he wanted to live? Why did both of us try so hard for so long to fight such a formidable foe? Why are loving moms and dads considered the "enemy" by our mental health system? Why are mental illness and our understanding and treatment of it still in the dark ages?

In the support group I run for families, one of the mothers mentioned a quote that goes something like, "A mother is as happy as her unhappiest child." When Pat was alive, my happiness was often impacted by his illness. When he was doing well,

I was doing well. When he was suffering—and let's be honest here, we really are talking about suffering—I found keeping my own balance challenging. How could I be grateful for all the good things in my life—my three wonderful daughters, my grandchildren, my friends, and every other blessing—when one of my offspring was in serious trouble?

I know it's not just me. I see how other mothers and grandmothers in our support group suffer, along with their ill children and grandchildren. If you haven't slogged down our path, there's no way you can get this. You stumble, blindfolded, through brambles and briars with a hole in your heart. Every minute. Every day.

Pat's ashes are in my living room high on a shelf where he can watch family gatherings. He always wanted to be home, and now he is. He loved his red electric guitar and his urn—it's really a handsome black box—has a three-dimensional electric red guitar on it. The inscription reads, "Pat, You Are the Music." When the time comes, my ashes will join his. And then, together, we'll rest beneath a giant redwood. A Pacific Coast forest will be our forever home.

Meanwhile, I'm tramping through the north's natural wonders. The Canadian Lakes—Moraine, Louise, Emerald, Peyto, and Bow—and mountains are varied and stunning. I walk on Athabasca Glacier at the Columbia Ice Fields. I descend to underground hot springs and ride a gondola high above Banff. I see Pat everywhere. I hope he sees me.

My son, Pat, was a sensitive poet with a ready wit. In my memoir, *Sooner Than Tomorrow—A Mother's Diary About Mental Illness, Family, and Everyday Life,* I've divided the sections by the seasons—summer/fall/winter/spring. I introduce each section with one of Pat's poems. The following is the poem for winter.

Tony's Finger

—PATRICK RANAHAN

He called the boiler room and said,
"This is John up in the penthouse.
Come on up and crack the steam in."
So I took the cowhide gloves and walked
across the January parking lot
to the main building of the hospital,
stuck my key in the elevator and rode it
to the mechanical penthouse, third floor.
The door opened to show me the tradesmen
all caught up on a different pipe
like kids on the monkey bars.
I put the pipe wrench to the blue valve
and cracked it slow, remembering John's admonition:
"You've got a hundred'n twenty pounds of pressure
coming through there. Open it too fast
and it'll blow you through the fucking roof."
Steam sang through the pipes as the condensate
dripped from the new silver gaskets
onto the concrete floor, scribbling a lazy map.
A man lost his finger here on the original job
putting in the permanent air handlers,
and when I look up to check the steam gauge,
I see where his buddies drew a picture—
a severed digit with the brotherly words:
"Hey Tony, here's your finger."

148

Holly Alston: "My son Terrell Scott. I am both sad and happy because this is a start of having Terrell's story heard. Thank you for including my Big Boy."

Margie Annis: "This is the last photo of my son Ronnie. It was taken several days before his death after I had cut his hair—unknowingly—for the last time."

149

April: "My brother and me."

Audrey Adams Auernheimer: "We have three
children who've been diagnosed with serious mental
illness. Two of them are deceased by suicide."

Joyce Berryman: "Me with one of my 19 grandchildren."

*Judy Waldo Bracken: "Me and my son, Ryland,
on a cool wintry day, January 2020."*

151

GG Burns: George Burns writes, "Wonderful wife, incredible mother, talented artist, and mental health pioneer. Now in heaven, with wings, painting the universe. So loved. So missed."

Leslie Carpenter: "Sometimes our advocacy takes years, sometimes months, but #RipplesOfHope do add up and make a difference."

*Sylvia Charters: "Jason Charters, RIP (1979-2020).
My son is gone but we must continue the fight for
all those who have been forgotten by society."*

*Jerri Clark: "Calvin and me on a Christmas Eve hike near
Seattle in 2018—15 months before his death from suicide."*

Elizabeth Courtois: "My daughter, Eva, at 11 years of age."

Ashley Doonan & Cathie Curtis: Ashley wrote, "I'm not sure what's worse: knowing that you have not and will not live up to your full potential, or knowing that it was never for lack of ability. Hemingway has his classic moment in The Sun Also Rises when someone asks Mike Campbell how he went bankrupt and all he can say is, 'gradually, then suddenly.'"

Donna Erickson: "Ryan's 2002 high school picture."

Heidi Franke: "This is my son, Mitchell, with his emotional suppport dog Indie. When he was 18, Mitchell said, 'Beauty is opinion. Art is life.' A bit esoteric but he is like a philosopher at times. I wish he would be well and could be a professor and teach many."

155

Deborah Harper: "Jared at 18 played his guitar, wrote songs, and played lacrosse. Within a year, he stopped bathing, slept on the floor, lived in a filthy room, and cursed out people we couldn't see or hear. He was 23 before we had an official diagnosis of schizophrenia."

Carole McAfee: "My son, Demian, and me."

Angela McCandless: "My son Dillon."

*Teresa Pasquini: "Advocating for Danny at
the California State Capitol."*

*Laura Pogliano: "My son Zaccaria Pogliano, age 16, in 2008.
He was stricken with schizophrenia later that year."*

*Linda Rippee Privatte/CJ Hanson: "This shows the
deteriorating condition we find our brother Mark living in
as a homeless person. We've attempted to care for him—
for the last 13 years—on the streets of his hometown."*

Dede Ranahan: "Pat and me (1969).
I can still feel him in my arms."

Ellie Shukert: "This is me, dressed as Dorothea Dix,
with San Francisco General psych nurses at City Hall
protesting the reduction of psychiatric beds in 2014."

Laurie Turley: "My sister, Carol, as a little girl."

Channin Henry Williams: "Raven and me when she was six. From an early age, Raven was passionate about picking and giving flowers. We began a tradition of decorating our home with all kinds of fresh-picked flowers—a tradition I have continued in her memory."

Cheri VanSant: "I am the mother of a beautiful son who lives with serious mental illness. This naturally pulls me toward others who struggle with SMI—like the friend in my story."

Pat Wood: "Brian (1979-2018).
My beloved son enjoying a concert."

I'm Prepared for Joey's Death

—REBECCA REINIG

I hope I can find some comfort in knowing I'm not alone.

My son Joey was just sent to Patton State Mental Hospital after spending seven months in San Diego County jail for trying to break into a car. (He'd been living in transient camps in San Diego County.) He makes $640 a month on SSI, not nearly enough to cover rent, basic needs, and food. He refuses to live at home because "I am an adult," and he doesn't want to be a burden.

At the jail, he was found incompetent to stand trial. I was reluctant about Patton, but hopeful that maybe he would receive some long-term help. And maybe, just maybe, he would receive the care and education he needs to maneuver this world as a person with serious mental illness, and to be at peace with the wonderfully different person he is.

Come to find out the only care and assistance Joey will receive, beyond medication, will be how to participate in court proceedings—not to yell out during court, not to speak unless spoken to—and how to understand the charges against him. That's it. No life skills, no education on his condition or how to recognize triggers, nothing. My son sleeps all day and doesn't have to participate in the court school, but that will make his stay longer.

My hopes were quickly deflated and we'll be in the same boat as prior to this arrest and many others. Joey will go to court, be found guilty of another felony, and released on time served (it's already been close to a year for a felony that, at the discretion of the court, could have been reduced to a misdemeanor because his attempt to break into the car failed). He will be released, again, to the streets. There is literally nowhere else for him to go—except home with us, which he refuses to do.

A vicious cycle. I'm prepared for Joey's death, which is the worst and most helpless feeling. I don't know what the answer is. I do know, for me, it's not over until he's at peace, healthy, and living the best life possible for him. He deserves at least that.

Our Pledge

—KAREN RICHES

"Goodby Jacob. I remember all the fun we had in this Volkswagen Beetle. I remember you sitting right there. I feel you. I feel like I'm leaving you because I just bought a new Beetle. I know it's not true. You and your brother and I put our thumbs together and pledged whoever was left would "Live their life." I think of that pledge many times a day. I love you both and miss both of you so. Love always, Your Mom"

I lost my son Jason to brain cancer. I lost Jacob because the ER thought he was lying about chest pain and because well, you know, "He has schizophrenia and all people with schizophrenia lie." He died in the ER, and the hospital wouldn't pick him up off the floor until he was blue.

The guards picked him up and dragged his body across the floor.

DOROTHEA DIX
REBORN

—ELLIE SHUKERT

I have two sons with mental illness and worry all the time that they could end up homeless when my husband and I are not around anymore. Or even before, as they are adults and a psychotic break could make them unresponsive to help.

I have so many friends in the same boat, friends made during 20 years of advocacy. I'm going to work until I die to motivate people in charge to develop a humane healthcare system with equal attention to serious mental illness (SMI). We've gotten as far as a determination, a few years ago, by the Supreme Court in Washington, DC, that people with SMI do qualify under the ADA for care, just like people in wheelchairs or with intellectual disabilities. Appropriate accommodations and care for them are required by law (San Francisco v. Sheehan).

Enforcement is the difficulty. Funding is the difficulty. Stigma. Ignorance. I hammer away on the computer, writing to politicians and the powers that be to do something help the SMI to get off the streets and out of prison, into the proper care and supportive housing. I wish I were a great novelist and could sway the public, but that power is a gift not enjoyed by many people.

I was just reading about Dorothea Dix's visit to the jail in Boston where they kept the female "lunatics" in the cold, damp basement with no heat throughout the winter. She got the mentally ill out of jails, cages, closets, and other locked basements. She shamed the legislature with her investigative journals and persuaded people to contribute money to build decent asylums with the humane treatments available at the time. All that, when women weren't supposed to speak in public (the 1840s and '50s).

I used to dress up like Dorothea at hearings at the city hall to draw attention to the tragedies playing out in San Francisco every day. Once, I pinned a photo onto my long black skirt of a young man with schizophrenia who had delusions of being followed by the CIA. He was trying to hide from "them" behind a bus. The bus driver didn't see him, backed up, and ran over him.

With only three minutes allowed to speak and our group scheduled to speak last, I hoped to wake the supervisors up to this needless accident that had taken place right outside their building. I found that the best use of such restricted time was to ask each of them what they would have me do if I found *them* helplessly sprawled on the sidewalk, delusional, psychotic, and in dire need of help.

"Would you have me call the police?" (You may be shot, especially if you have anything that resembles a weapon—so few officers have the training, patience, or the ability to deal with the SMI and will plead in their defense that there was a danger to themselves or others.)

"Would you want me to just walk on by and ignore your distress?"

"Or, if there were a mobile crisis team available (the big if), wouldn't you prefer that I called trained, empathetic mental health professionals to come and help you figure out the next step. Perhaps contact your doctor or take you to a psych ER if you are a danger to yourself or others?"

I knew the supervisors wouldn't answer, but they did seem pensive.

Some people "get it" and some don't. I keep reaching out for the people in power who do want to provide humane and evidence-based care for the SMI. One day, we'll get to the tipping point. But it's a tug of war. A big step would be to reform the entire healthcare system and make it available to all Americans for every illness, so I'm pushing for national, universal, or Medicare for all—whatever you want to call it. Also, for more subsidized, supportive housing.

It might be the one good thing that comes from this pandemic—the realization that nobody will stay healthy unless the healthcare (including mental healthcare) umbrella covers all of us. Thanks to everyone out there who is trying so hard. I'm grateful to all of you. You're not alone. I'm not alone. It helps.

A Mother's Request
in Court

—KAT SHULTZ

Here is the statement Kat made to the judge at her son's sentencing:

I have to begin by expressing how profoundly sorry I am for the severe trauma and loss that Melissa, John, Evan, and the rest of their family and friends have suffered, but words don't even exist to express it adequately. It is only on the advice of attorneys, concerned with both the criminal and civil cases filed, that I have not reached out to you, which goes against every fiber of my being. So many people were catastrophically affected by this tragedy and not a single day goes by that I don't think about the agony it's caused for you and pray for your healing.

There never was any "good" outcome to this trial. Nothing decided here will take away the suffering we've had to endure, the pain that we all continue to feel or the resulting hardships we must now face. This can never be undone for our families. It would have been difficult enough for my son to accept having a serious brain illness had he gotten the treatment we were so desperately seeking, but the remorse over what he's done to a family he loves, because of his illness, will haunt him forever. However, just maybe, by shattering the silence, indifference, and lack of understanding surrounding serious mental illness and our failing mental health industry, we can effect change that will help the next families in crisis. This is the only way to bring about justice now.

The human brain is like any other organ in the body—able to benefit from healthy habits while still susceptible to injury, disease and illness. Yet we don't treat people with brain illness like we treat those with serious illness in other parts of the body. Imagine your child comes home with a severely broken arm, calling the doctor and being told you'll have to wait three months for an appointment. Or being sent home from the emergency room without treatment or medication and having doctors tell you that you'll have to set it yourself.

Whereas a broken bone is evidenced by pain, swelling, maybe even bent or protruding bones, the brain controls (among all other bodily functions) our thoughts, reasoning, and behaviors. Serious brain illnesses, such as schizophrenia spectrum disorders, manifest themselves through strange, unpredictable, and often violent or criminal behaviors. The sufferer is shunned, denied treatment, and very often ends up incarcerated. Everyone who cares about or is victimized by them suffers. This has to change, and none of us is safe until it does.

When this horrible tragedy first happened, the public defender went in front of the television cameras and said she had no doubt that this was a case of serious mental illness, and she was absolutely right. The prosecuting attorney also went before the cameras, saying how we aren't even safe in our own homes anymore, and he was also right—though I don't believe he fully understood or appreciates why.

During my son's trial, we heard five different doctors, experts in the field of forensic psychology and psychiatry, who spent about 60 hours evaluating him, come up with closely related diagnoses all within the schizophrenia family of illnesses. They referred to my son's as a "textbook case," and no other motive whatsoever was presented for his crime, because there is none. This tragedy was caused by the inaction of our police officers and county mental health emergency services, and could have been prevented.

Two fallacies are most frequently offered as excuses for this inaction. The first is the pretentious claim that it's out of respect for my son's civil rights. When the responding officer refused to arrest him on an involuntary 5150 hold, and I told him that I thought his trying to walk to South America barefoot did constitute "a danger to himself," the officer callously responded (and I quote), "If your 18-year-old son wants to walk to South America barefoot and live in the jungle, that's his right!"

When any sane person considers what has become of Jordy's or my son's civil rights now by denying him treatment before tragedy, this argument shows itself to be blatantly irrational.

The second false excuse is that there aren't enough resources, in terms of staff and facilities, to properly treat those with serious mental illness, and that to do so would be too costly. All research shows that not providing these services leads to much greater costs to the communities at large. You don't need to read the research (as I have done) to know this. Just consider the ridiculous cost of this trial. The expert witness fees for the five doctors alone amounted to an excess of $50,000 or $60,000. There are so many other unseen costs as well, resulting from the lack of treatment and incarceration of the mentally ill, not the least of which are the human costs in loss of life, loss of productivity, and suffering.

In order to move forward, I've had to struggle with so much anger over the fact that, when I suspected that my son was suffering from a serious brain illness and I called for help, I was dismissed as a "hysterical mom." Even though I'd explained, as calmly and respectfully as possible to the responding officer, that I'd lost my eldest child to suicide just two years earlier and my son had already had a serious psychotic episode just six weeks prior. No one who knew my son could ever have imagined him capable of what he did. He'd only been known to be a kind and highly respectful young man, who's never even been in a fight in school. My greatest fear, at that time, was that he'd end up among our countless homeless on the streets and I'd never see him again.

To add insult to injury, I come to find out that this officer has been off work receiving worker's compensation (factor that into the cost of all this) because of this incident, while all the rest of us have had to find a way to pick up the pieces and go back to work.

As wrong as he was, I have already forgiven this officer because I have a great appreciation for what our officers are being forced to deal with on a daily basis. My own father is a retired San Diego County Sheriff's homicide detective who retired with severe job-related depression, and my grandfather is a retired Riverside County Sheriff, who also taught criminology in San Francisco. They were two of the first people I called when my son was arrested. It was my grandfather, now in his 80s, who told me that when he was a Riverside sheriff in the '50s and '60s, they had a squad they unofficially referred to as the "psycho" squad. However un-P.C. that name may be today, they were specially trained to deal with people suffering from mental illness, to de-escalate situations, to apprehend them peacefully, and once they did, they had a place to take them to get help. And this happened often enough that they had an entire squad for it. That kind of training and those treatment facilities don't exist anymore.

As I was researching our current state of affairs, I got hold of the catalog of offerings for the American Correctional Association's 2015 Annual Summer Conference in hopes of finding something encouraging. When I turned to the section related to mental illness, all I found was a session titled, "How to Bullet-proof Yourself Against Litigation."

While too many news stories these days point to the obvious need for better officer education and training around responding to people with mental illness, placing all of the responsibility on them is unfair and unwise. Having voluntarily gone to Contra Costa Regional Medical Center for an evaluation, my son was not taken seriously, even though he was clearly delusional. And even though he signed the paperwork in the ambulance before he left, putting me under the HIPAA umbrella, I was not contacted in order to give them a more complete psychiatric history until they had already put him in a taxi.

After I found out he had been discharged after such a brief time, I asked to speak to a psychiatrist in charge. I explained the situation and once again was treated with disdain. When I asked for advice or possibly medications, I was offered absolutely nothing. When I asked if I could come pick him up, I was told he had already been sent home in a cab. Our treatment facilities must start including families when making diagnoses and stop relying solely on those whose brains aren't functioning right to provide critical information and make decisions regarding their own well-being.

I've been teaching since 1991 and have worked with thousands of students and their families. Serious mental illnesses like schizophrenia affect, at the very least, five percent of the population, meaning hundreds of those families have faced the same difficulties, and I can't help but imagine what horrors they went through or where they are now. Today, I cannot go into my fourth grade classroom and look at my young students without wondering *who's next?* Justice for Jordy requires that we acknowledge the failures that led to his horrific death and do whatever we can to fix things before more and more tragedies like this occur.

The keys to overcoming any great tragedy or challenge are forgiveness and gratitude—forgiveness, because it unblocks the path to understanding and change, and gratitude, because it gives us the strength to carry on. Sometimes the only gratitude to be found is for the opportunity to grow stronger and bring about change for having been through the ordeal. I am so grateful for the huge amount of support, compassion, and understanding we've received from our local community, and from the rapidly growing community of families going through similar experiences around the country. Since this happened, I've been welcomed into a number of private, secret groups. Some of these groups have been established to provide comfort and assistance, while others are focused on political action to bring about policy changes. These groups are secret for many reasons, probably the greatest of which is the fear of public perception of the mentally ill.

As far as my son's sentencing, I would like to respectfully request just one thing from the court. I've already lost one child to suicide and my son Billy has attempted it twice within this detention facility. All research shows that the risk of suicide increases dramatically with both lack of treatment and incarceration. I ask that Your Honor order that all the doctors' notes, evaluations, and test results be included as part of my son's permanent psychiatric record to follow him wherever he is sent, and that he may receive appropriate care in order to prevent further suffering and death in our family.

Thank you, Your Honor, for allowing me this time and listening to me.

Note: The judge found Kat's son, who suffers from serious mental illness, guilty of murder and sentenced him to prison for 30 years to life.

I'm Never Calling the Crisis Team or the Police Again

—KECIA BOLKEN SPECK

Oh my goodness! I'm never calling the crisis team or the police again.

This morning my son had a really, really rough time. He was calling and texting me, his grandma, his psych doc, and several members of the ACT team (all the people who are supposed to be supporting him and who we tell him to call if he is in distress).

He was distraught because he believes that I, his mom, killed somebody in 1984. He texted me and said, "You need to cry and feel pain." So I was advised by the ACT team to call the crisis number and to have the police do a well check on him. The police said that they were really busy today but that they would try to get to him tomorrow. They did, however, advise me not to go near him.

The crisis team said that because nobody's seen a weapon, and because my son didn't actually threaten me or threaten to harm himself (well not today, but yesterday he did), that they would document my call, but there was nothing else they could do.

Now the ACT team has called and they're too scared to take meds to my severely mentally ill son. They're going to scale back on their assistance until they feel safer sending workers to his apartment.

So my son has to go without meds during his delusional psychotic breakdown? Who will take his insulin shot to him? The police have advised me not to have contact with him. What now? My poor son's distraught and will not get his meds.

Update: My hands are shaking as I type this.

My son is an inpatient and willingly taking Abilify orally. It's been several days now, and he's responding really well to it. Although he continues to have disorganized speech and some delusional thinking, he no longer wants to make me cry and feel pain.

I am so strong during the hard parts. Since the "worst" is over, for now, I am falling apart. All of those same feelings from the very beginning of this nightmare six years ago are coming back. Some of you know them so well. This is the time, today, right this minute, that I really should have a doctor appointment for myself. It seems that my doctor sees me hold it together so often and for so long that he doesn't think I need help. Compliments from everyone all the time—"I don't know how you do it." "I'm not as strong as you." "I couldn't do it."

Really? Because who else will do it? Today, I'm going to stay in my pajamas, drink my coffee, and cry and mourn the loss of my son. And the loss of myself.

Finding Sarah

—JOANN STRUNK

Thirteen days after walking away from her adult day care program, my daughter was found as she wandered out of the woods not far from where she went missing. She'd never been more than two miles from town the whole time. Someone saw her and recognized her as the missing woman. She was taken to the hospital in Fort Thomas—about an hour away. She was dehydrated to the point that her kidneys were shutting down.

Sarah says she left after a disagreement with someone. She felt that the whole town was screaming at her to go away and die. She walked through some woods and crossed the river (which is very possible because it is way down). She became lost in woods on the other side. She became convinced that the world had ended and she was the only one left alive. So she gave up.

Can you imagine being so psychotic and hallucinating and lost in the woods? She could find some water but no food. When she finally decided to try to save herself she was almost too weak to walk. Thank God she decided to try. The search teams had been very close to her. She heard people calling her name but thought it wasn't real. We were so close and missed her. It will take a while to forgive myself for that.

The director of her group home told me he didn't believe her, that she couldn't have survived out there that long. He thinks she's lying to protect whoever she was with. But I'm inclined to think it's true. I've never seen anyone so dirty. Her neck was green. It looked like mold beginning to grow. She was wearing the clothes she went missing in, and they are in tatters. Her hair was one dreadlock with sticks and burrs, and she was dehydrated to the point of death.

She told me that she's learned how easy it can be to die. She said she'd abandoned her things at some point. So why did her messenger show activity on Monday? A mystery. I'm going to go try to find her things soon and to get to the bottom of what happened. Right now I'm just being here with her. The rest will sort itself out.

I am so sad. So infinitely sad at what our sick loved ones have to bear. Sarah's life has been an unbelievable horror and the torment in her mind is even worse. We, as a society, are failing them so badly.

"They Should Have Let You Help Me. I Wasn't in My Right Mind"

—LAURIE TURLEY

Butterly & This Is My Heart, Take Care

—CAROL A. SNYDER

My sister Carol was a high honors student in high school, graduating valedictorian in her senior class, and receiving a full scholarship to an ivy-league university to study journalism. Something happened while she was away at school, but my brother and I, being several years younger, weren't privy to the hushed conversations between my parents and older siblings about just what was the matter. I knew Carol could be volatile and prone to outbursts of anger and irrational reasoning. I also knew she was creative and full of ideas about the world, which I found intriguing and inspiring.

I left home at 17 when I went to college. I never really lived with my family after that, only returning home to visit on holidays. By then, my sister was living with a man with whom she bore a son. She held jobs—a staff writer for a magazine; a writing teacher at the local university. She wrote poetry, beautiful poetry. Writing and books were her love and her life. While family gatherings were often uncomfortable and awkward when she was around, I wasn't present to witness the worst of her behaviors, so I was unaware of just how seriously ill she was. I only knew she was "different," but I loved her, loved her writing, loved her creativity, and loved my sister for herself.

It wasn't until several years later, after I had married, lived three states away, and my second child was an infant in my arms, that my mother called to tell me that they had to have Carol committed to the state psychiatric hospital. Just like mother's own brother, my uncle, my sister was involuntarily admitted to the same state hospital where he had lived many years before his death. I learned that my sister had inherited the family illness: schizophrenia.

Details of the years following that first hospitalization are sketchy, at least from what I knew. On trips home to visit the family, I visited my sister in the hospital, in her home, and in the mental health outpatient center where she introduced me to her friends. I cried with her when her 12-year-old son was removed from her home by Child Protective Services and put into foster care, where none of us were able to see him—due to legal restrictions and "conflict of interest" in our relationship with her. I rejoiced with her when she finally agreed to stay on medication, and when she found a psychiatrist who was willing to work with her—in her words, "Like a tinker, an alchemist"— until they found just the right combination of medication that would keep her stable for the next 20 years.

Even though she was medically stable, Carol still struggled daily to find her place in a world that couldn't see this woman— whom I knew as a beautiful soul—as anything other than a mentally ill person. Medication would keep her stable, but she never could recover, and never be free of schizophrenia and many of the symptoms that medication could not erase. Sometimes the medication would fail and need to be readjusted, and she would regress. She aged prematurely, lost her teeth, was at times morbidly obese, and at others less so, often had a dulled expression, developed diabetes, and was violently assaulted in her own apartment by someone who took nothing from her but the medication she had in her purse.

Yet, through it all, she maintained her generous nature and her creative drive to write poetry and fiction. I collaborated with her on compiling some of her poems into a hardcover book with my photographs accompanying them. In the spring before she died, we self-published several copies to give to friends and family, and she was even able to sell a few. It had always been her dream to be published, and even though this wasn't the same as having her poems accepted by a large publishing company, she told me that she felt her dream had come true. It was the last good thing I was able to do for her.

A few years before Carol died, we began having long phone conversations. I was struggling with a crisis within my own family, and she alone was willing to listen any time, day or night, as I asked her probing questions to help me understand. She generously shared with me insights into her illness, and tried to help me understand what was impossible to comprehend. She would talk me through many of my darkest times, having a firsthand knowledge of the grief and helplessness that comes of seeing someone you love suffer. She was wise, giving, and forgiving. She was my rock of wisdom and support during those phone calls. At the other end of the line, when she spoke to me, my sister was complete and whole.

I visited her in her brand new apartment, which had been subsidized and furnished by charitable agencies. It was bright, with high ceilings, wood floors, and big windows, with two bedrooms and clean furniture that had been provided for her. I stayed a weekend with her. We cooked meals together, went shopping together, and she talked about wanting to teach a writing class again. I had every hope and reason to believe that my sister was going to thrive.

A little less than a year later, Carol began to sound halting in our phone conversations, and would sometimes ramble without direction, or her speech would be slurred. She told me that she had begun to hear voices again, and that she was afraid she needed to have her medication adjusted. I encouraged her to do so soon. She promised me she would. She shared that she hadn't seen her psychiatrist in some time, but was going to make an appointment.

I now know that she probably never followed through. I believe that she had regressed too far into the illness to be able to make that rational choice of action on her own. Severe mental illnesses such as schizophrenia take away a person's ability to reason clearly.

My own life situation took a dreadful turn, and I was preoccupied with trying to cope with things at home, so I didn't get down to visit her that whole next year. When I finally did, nearly a year after she had moved into her new apartment, I found Carol lying asleep on her couch. Her apartment had gone from a comfortable, homey, bright space to rooms full of clutter so deep I could hardly make my way through. Unwashed dishes and molding food filled the sink and covered the stove. Dirty laundry and dirty counter and table-tops added filthy, unsanitary conditions. How did this occur? I had to get help for her. With the help of her now-adult son and some other siblings, I got the numbers of her case manager and her former treatment providers. Not one of them would talk with me except to say, "Your sister is her own guardian and has the right to refuse treatment," which apparently she did. Each and every one of them told me that she was entitled to make her own choices and there was nothing I or anyone else could do.

I knew, because she'd told me, that she feared being sent "back up to the Hill," which the state psychiatric hospital was called. I knew she feared being in a locked ward and forced into treatment. I knew she'd lapsed into a state of psychotic illness, and I couldn't prevent her downfall nor convince her that treatment, voluntary or involuntary, was exactly what she desperately needed.

A visiting nurse knocked on the door while I was there, to deliver insulin which my sister was responsible for administering to herself. The nurse tested her blood sugar levels. They were way above normal. While my sister sat outside on the deck and stabbed her arm with the needle of insulin the nurse had given her, I took the nurse into the apartment. Amidst the filth, we discovered several vials of unopened insulin, evidence that she hadn't taken her diabetes medication and, of course, it was obvious that she hadn't taken her anti-psychotic medication. I begged the nurse to please help me help my sister. It was obvious Carol needed to be on medication and back into treatment. I thought, if I could just make her look around and acknowledge my sister was in need, surely she would file a report and help me get my sister into treatment. The nurse said what every other care provider I'd called for the past month said: "Your sister is clearly in need, but she's her own guardian and, if she refuses treatment, there is nothing anyone can do."

I left my sister in that horrible state, in that unsanitary, unsafe condition, with my heart broken. I returned home, promising her I was going to continue to call her and stay in touch. I promised myself I wouldn't give up trying to persuade someone—anyone—to get her out of there and into treatment.

A week or two later, I received a phone call from Carol's son that she'd been taken by ambulance to the hospital with a serious and invasive lung infection. She was in medical care for several weeks, during which time, back on psychiatric medication, her ability to reason began to return, even while her physical health continued to decline. In one of our last phone conversations, Carol shared that she felt life returning within her, that she felt like she was awakening from a bad dream. She said to me, "I don't know how I got so bad. I was doing so well. How did things get so bad?" I told her we all knew she was going downhill and we tried to help her, but she refused help. There was nothing family members could do. Her next words were among the last she ever spoke to me. "They should have let you help me. I wasn't in my right mind."

"They should have let you help me. I wasn't in my right mind."

Not long after that conversation, the illness in my sister's lungs, which I have no doubt began as a result of the unhealthy condition of her apartment, progressed into a severe pneumonia. Despite the doctors' efforts, they couldn't clear her of the infection. After a week of intensive care, it developed into sepsis and took her life.

All our efforts to rescue her from descending back into the illness she couldn't manage on her own had been futile. It took an invasive lung infection to get her back on anti-psychotic medication, but it was too late to save her life. The laws designed to protect her civil rights were the very laws that prevented those who loved her most from helping her when she was unable to help herself.

"They should have let you help me. I wasn't in my right mind."

Those words will haunt me until the end of my days. Those words are why I believe that families need to be listened to. Families, regardless of whether they have legal guardianship or not, should have the right to get their loved ones to humane and sound mental health treatment when they see the need. They're the ones who see the signs first and most clearly.

My sister's untimely death is why I believe that so many, who are left to "die with their rights on," are rather, in truth, denied their right to live because of our current restrictive laws. Carol's last words to me continue to be my inspiration. They inspire me to fight for treatment for the seriously mentally ill who are unable to help themselves.

"They should have let you help me. I wasn't in my right mind."

BUTTERFLY

—CAROL A. SNYDER

Butterfly, stay away from my net,
It's there on the ground.
I will not pick it up.
I will not chase after you as others do.
I would chase your colors, lovely lemons,
Butters, purples, monarch's orange
and blacks away from the flowers
that others would snap their nets over.
Send you after the freedom
that you surely deserve.
I do not like being trapped.
Why should you?

THIS IS MY HEART, TAKE CARE

—CAROL A. SNYDER

Because you're probably going to squeeze my heart like clay,
I make it mud and send it to the river
to wash clean over stone and pebbles
to make it blue and green as the river water
fresh and sweet as river-rinsed air
And hope you'll see it, what the river pours forth, as good.
Even though you'll probably never recognize me.
Even then, I wish this good for you.

"He Has Schizophrenia, Your Honor"

—SANDY TURNER

Once upon a time, when Casey was very sick and demonstrating symptoms of his illness in the courtroom, his overwhelmed public defender started defending Casey by speaking out on an entirely different case. I raised my hand and said, "He has the wrong file, Your Honor."

A large bailiff came near to me, so I apologized and slunk down. When his defender began speaking again, it was as if he was speaking from a routine script with no sense of what was happening to this beautiful young man's life. My son was disappearing right before my eyes.

I raised my hand again and said, "He has schizophrenia, Your Honor."

The large bailiff came and stood in front of me again, this time with his arms crossed in front of him. I apologized a second time and watched as this amazing judge got it. The prosecutor finally got it, too, and came to speak with me. I asked, "Why do they prosecute patients for displaying symptoms of their illness?" He put his head down and shook it.

Just one day in our trip down behavioral lane. I remember every one of them.

Casey Alan Campbell
October 29, 1985—October 1, 2009

Those beautiful days. Our fairytales did not end well. But, oh Dede, the beautiful days we had with these amazing loves are forever. So loving and aware of others. I sometimes looked at Casey and thought to myself, *Where did you come from, you beautiful-hearted little soul?*

Why Is This Okay?

—SHARON UNDERWOOD

My son Tim has been homeless, staying with friends or couch surfing, since he turned 18 (24 now). The minute he turned 18, he walked away from his supported-living group home. He can't live with me. I can't control him. He refuses all forms of therapy, including meds, and blocks me from all legal and medical information. He demands money, thinks I injected him with poison to make him sick, and believes I'm withholding a nonexistent trust fund from him. I'm out of work and broke. Real broke. Barely making it broke. I've been giving my son at least $100–200 a month as he won't apply for SSI because he thinks that's how the demons will track him. He says, "I'm not sick."

The doctors have diagnosed my son with schizoaffective disorder. He self-medicates with whatever substance he can get his hands on, has been arrested 40 times, and has a felony assault charge against a police officer. I've tried to get him committed (for at least long enough to get him some help) for six years with no luck. He tells authorities he's not suicidal or dangerous and they let him go. I love him so much, but he's prone to disturbingly scary behaviors and I've had to get restraining orders on the advice of his doctor.

Last week, my fiancée and I were driving home from the grocery store and saw my son coming from my house. We stopped to talk with him. He was pissed. He said, "I put a hole in your garage door, and the landlord called the police." I reminded him, "You can't come over and get me into trouble." He basically told me, "You don't care about me," and he fled on foot. I pulled up the street into my parking lot. My son had smashed my fiancée's truck, over and over, into the garage door. He caused $5000 worth of damage. The truck wasn't touched, due to a customized front end. The police picked him up down the street.

I'm losing everything. My fiancée is wonderful and my landlords are trying to be helpful. I filed for a new restraining order and plan to move. I feel like my son's left me no choice. He's in jail and will be for a while. I don't know if I'm relieved to not be terrorized every day or profoundly struck with heartbreak and guilt. I'm now $5000 in debt and have, for all intents and purposes, lost my son. I'm sick of this terrible disease. I'm sick of the terrible system that governs it. The cops all know he's sick. The doctors all know he's sick. The judges all know he's sick. I can't believe my sick son can be left to his own devices. I can't believe that the only treatment he'll get will be in jail or prison.

Why is this okay? Tim talks like he's 10 years old. How is this okay?

My relationship with my son is now damaged beyond repair. I'm heartbroken and scared to death of him, and all because of the law. It says, basically, my son has to kill someone in order to be committed and properly treated and evaluated.

I don't know if I'll ever be okay in my heart.

Update: Since Tim's arrest in Oregon for unauthorized use of a motor vehicle, he's spent two months waiting for a spot in Oregon State Hospital. I've been in contact with his probation officer as well as the district attorney because I was a witness to my fiancée's truck being taken. We've been assured that, in Oregon, a crime with mental health issues is treated differently. A new order was designed to assist a mentally ill suspect in being evaluated, treated (mandatory treatment if necessary in an attempt to get him fit for trial), and transitioned out of jail or the hospital.

On a Saturday night, I got a message from the Automatic Defendant Tracking System (VINES) saying my son was released from jail. The jail's phone line wasn't open on the weekend, so I waited until Monday and called the district attorney, who assured me that Tim was finally transported to the state hospital, and he would be there at least 30 days—possibly a year or more— determined by his evaluation and needed treatment.

So, ten days later, there was a knock at the door at 8:00 a.m. It woke my fiancée and me up. It was my son. We had a restraining order and my fiancée, shook up and barely awake, reminded Tim he couldn't be on the property. Tim ran. I called the police, but they couldn't find him. I called the probation officer. She called me back seven hours later. My son had been released from jail instead of being transported to the state hospital. He was told he was free and instructed to show up in court on January 15, 2020.

Apparently, the jail made the mistake, and now, no one knows where Tim is. There are warrants out for his arrest, but the police can't find him. I live in Medford, Oregon, a tiny 80,000-person town. Not Portland. Not LA. My fiancée and I have been to every shelter and homeless outreach and driven to areas known to homeless people. My son is nowhere. Just nowhere.

I didn't know he'd been released and was half asleep when he came by. If I'd known that his release was accidental (and didn't just feel that, once again, they'd let him fall through the cracks), I'd have possibly done something different that morning. My fiancée and I are sick that that might have been our last chance to get him into the state hospital. It's 30 degrees here at night right now. I feel angry and guilty for trusting the system. I feel helpless at the same time.

As I write, my son is out there with no help. I'm going to check some places again. I feel like I have to find him myself because the police can't. Or won't.

If you Google "Aid and Assist" in Oregon, you'll see the services they claim to provide—serving time in the state hospital getting help, transitioning through aftercare, housing assistance. Our family was so happy and hopeful for what that meant. We all thought Tim might get his meds back and have help filing for disability. Instead, every day or other day, I go to the drug dealing park, or to the soup kitchen, or to the shelter. I try to spot Tim so the police can get called and we can continue back to what was supposed to happen in the first place.

I'm sad. I'm scared for and of him. I'm so disgusted with the system and that I have to do everything myself and, if don't find him, I'll be the terrible parent. The terrible person. I can't ask anyone to help anymore. They just won't. It's on me.

We Need Holistic Health Care for People With SMI

—CHERI VANSANT

My friend from church with serious mental illness (SMI), was hospitalized for severe depression about eight weeks ago. She is 67 years old and has managed her illness very well for many years. This time, however, she appeared to be having neurological symptoms that were unusual for her.

With no family of her own, I, as just a friend who's also an RN, had no clout in suggesting a neurological consult. The hospital psychiatrist agreed she needed to be seen by a neurologist, but for some reason that didn't happen. After a week in the hospital, she was stabilized, psychiatrically, and sent home.

After returning home, my friend had a seizure and was taken to the ER, where an MRI was done. The MRI showed that she has a massive brain tumor (growing for at least 30 years) that's operable but still very dangerous to remove surgically.

Why didn't someone do an MRI scan when my friend's symptoms first appeared? Why do healthcare professionals think that SMI patients' problems are always psych problems? Holistic healthcare was the mantra when I was in nursing school. We were told to look at the complete person, but that's not my observation in the medical world today. People with psychiatric brain disorders are treated differently.

I'm so sad, tonight, that I didn't fight harder for my sweet friend. It's so important that we caregivers demand better overall healthcare for our loved ones.

No one cares about crazy people.

Prepare Myself?
How Do I Do That?

—FRANCIE VANZANDT

It's morning, nearly 9:30 a.m. I finally got a little sleep, which gets harder each day for me and for my son, my only surviving son (three others have passed away—different story). He is again incarcerated in the county jail—seven, maybe eight times this year for a few hours, a couple days, two weeks, 45 days. This time his sentence is one year. Yes, an entire year. He has suffered several years being diagnosed bi-polar, schizophrenic, dual diagnosis. Words—I had no idea what they meant. I didn't believe it could be even true. After all, those people he called "his doctors," they didn't know my son. Not like I did. All of his 23 years. They just gave him pills that made him so out of it. He learned how to manipulate some of his doctors to get more and more meds. To stay as far out there as he needed to quiet the voices he said were screaming at him.

Only he could see and hear them. I was a liar. Dude continuously accused me because I couldn't hear them. I couldn't. I honestly tried to listen with him late in the night and in the wee hours of morning as he paced the floor and covered all the windows to "secure" our home. He spent endless hours, days, and nights screwing the closet doors and windows closed so whoever was in there—or out there—couldn't get to him or me. He wanted to protect me. I wanted to protect him from himself. I didn't then and still don't know how. "That's who needs to be in jail," he justified. "They want to harass me. They hate me. I'm not good enough."

You know what I'm talking about. We lived together April 2014 through December 2018. We shared the big country home that once belonged to my grandparents, then to my parents, and finally was going to be the forever home for Dude and me. The first year was pretty amazing. We were excited to be living in the home we had both grown up in, although in different eras. We shared ideas and worked together on restoration projects, singing and laughing as we worked side by side. His great pride was that we were a "team." He tried hard to cut back on meds and overmedicating, which I blamed for his rough days or nights. I blamed his doctors, his adolescent drug experimenting, his motorcycle accident (another failed suicide attempt), anything. I needed someone to blame for the craziness I couldn't believe was happening. It was definitely happening.

Last night, I scheduled and paid for a video visitation at the jail to spend 15 minutes with my son face-to-face. He had an audience of four or five fellow, rather disrespectful, inmates looking over his shoulder just behind him in the crowded space they share. We had no privacy. As Dude looked me in the eyes he said, "How are you, Mom? You are beautiful, Mom." I said, "Thank you, Dude. I'm doing okay. I love you." He stared at me for a long, silent moment. I saw no joy in his eyes, only fear and sadness. He was lost and broken. Breaking the intense silence, he turned as if to hide from his audience and said very clearly, "I told you I can't do this, Mom. I won't get out of here the same. I won't be the same. Prepare yourself. I have to go now, Mom. I love you, too." Then the screen went blank.

I am sobbing as I type, recalling our four-minute video visit.

The home we shared is in a small, rural area with local cops with small-town mentality. Not much to do but cruise the few streets looking for lights on after 10:00 p.m. Something must be going on. A knock at the door. Dude politely opens it and an officer pushes his way in. This sends Dude into panic mode. Delusional, he begins to get defensive. Dude knows, because of his accident and a couple other suicide attempts, he is on probation. The police assume his behavior is drug or alcohol related. He does neither. Refusing to pee in front of anyone and exposing himself to embarrassing humiliation by a stranger in uniform gets him a free ride to the jail 50 miles away. The ride allows entertainment and occupies the bored, big, bad, badge-wearing officer for the evening. I've witnessed the police getting him out of bed—"Pee for us, Dude."

If that's not harassment, what is? The charge is probation violation. Refusing to test. Well, it appears to me the judge is not aware of what mental illness is or does to a family. I have learned so much in the past eight months since I moved to Fairfield, California. I work for Solano County IHHS (In-Home Health Services). My first client is Catherine Rippee-Hanson. She and I spend hours talking about her brother, my son, and the many others who suffer with SMI. I've read the book, *Sooner Than Tomorrow*, twice. Thank you. I'm enlightened and now know that I don't need to accept blame at all anymore. Mental illness just is. It's not Dude's fault or mine or his doctors' or anything. It just is.

I'm learning to understand and educate myself and our family about what has alienated my son from all of his siblings and his father. It is me and Dude. I'm so glad he is my son. I pray that God hears me when I sometimes cry out helplessly overwhelmed. That's when I remember you and your son, Dede, and your words of wisdom through experiences so similar to mine. I'm thankful for the many ways your book has changed me and the way I think and manage my life. I can't begin to thank you enough.

I am so blessed that my son (against the odds) is still with me. Prepare myself? How do I do that?

"Please Don't Kill My Son"

—DARLENE BEEN WATKINS

My wonderful, heavenly angel son, Shane Watkins (39), was shot by a Lawrence County deputy because he thought all people with mental illness were dangerous. My son called 911 saying I threatened to kill him and his dog. I told 911, "We have no guns in the house and please tell the cop not to kill my son."

When the cop got out of his truck, he had his gun in his hand. I was standing in the doorway. My son was standing by my car. I begged the cop, "Please don't kill my son." Not even five-seconds later, he shot my son three times in the chest. One bullet went into the hood of my car. Then he pointed the gun at me and threatened to kill me, too.

The police report stated that I said my son attacked me, but he didn't. The police report said my son attacked the cop, but he didn't. I'm still praying for justice and still waiting to get another court date. The last one was cancelled.

I just came to the cemetery to put flowers and Alabama memorabilia on Shane's grave. Since he loved steak, I'll eat a steak in honor of his life.

My love and prayers for all the mothers who have lost a child. Thank you for your support and for sharing your losses.

Please Help
Find Ryan

—CHRISTI WEEKS

I went to visit Ryan at St Luke's tonight at 6:30 p.m., and three staff members came out and informed me Ryan went AWOL from an off-unit activity that started at 3:15 p.m. Ryan wasn't discovered missing until 4:30 p.m. I have one missed call from St Luke's Hospital at 4:36 p.m. No voicemail message. No other attempts to call me.

The staff didn't call the Community Bridges on-call case manager from Ryan's forensic ACT team. The police didn't respond to take a missing person report until 6:30 p.m. In fact, the police were leaving the hospital as I was arriving to visit. I questioned the staff about the two-hour lag in contact with the police and was told this wasn't an emergency.

Ryan is on court-ordered treatment on Clozapine. And this is not an emergency?

(Clozapine has a short 12-hour half life, meaning it is completely cleared from the brain within 12 hours, and can have a rapid onset of withdrawal if abruptly stopped. Abrupt withdrawal of clozapine has been associated with symptoms of "cholinergic rebound," including nausea, vomiting, hyper-salivation, diarrhea, diaphoresis, insomnia, and agitation, as well as rapid onset of psychosis. Clozapine

is usually only prescribed for people who don't respond well to other antipsychotic drugs, and is prescribed with caution because of potentially dangerous side effects and acute withdrawal effects.)

I will hold this hospital accountable. I can't believe this. Ryan is still missing. I contacted his team at Community Bridges and they are outreaching to try to find him tonight. Please keep Ryan in your prayers.

Walk a Mile in Our Shoes

—KIMBERLEE COOPER WEST

Walk a mile in our shoes. Our children are rarely mentioned. In the circles we travel, people pretend our son is nonexistent. Something, anything would be better than nothing. It would be so nice to have the same privileges as those who have medical diseases. People do not understand our kids. They do have a medical disease.

Tonight, I watched a new show called "Human First." Halfway through, I started crying after seeing the enormous help for patients with physical illnesses. The amazing support patients receive at the NIH hospital are incredible. No one complains about their high-priced therapies.

People complain about people with mental disorders using up too many resources. We pay insurance like everyone else. Why are our services rationed? Or we hear, "Well, we can't help everybody." Insinuating medical services would run out due to us? Where is our place to drop off sick kids? Where are our research studies? When do they receive hospitalization and treatment? If only they would add up the Department of Justice bill.

Why is it okay to torture our children with jail and prison? My son has been in jail since February, 18, 2017. He was in a hospital. Within five days of release, he was arrested. He was so unstable he ended up in solitary confinement for almost two weeks.

One good thing is my son's coming to terms with his own race. After being called the "n" word at school (fairly sure it triggered this last episode), Ty said, "Mama, no, really, I'm not black. I'm white." We hired Sedrick, his African American counselor, to help him with this. Then Ty fired Sedrick.

We'd tell Ty, "We love every black bone in your body." He called last week to inform us, "I use grease now. My bunkmate, Larry, (who is black) showed me how." We said, "We're so happy to hear that." One upside is I think his racial identity crisis is finally cured.

In the meantime, my son's treated like a maximum security prisoner in a county jail. He's locked in thirty hours at a time. He hasn't had exercise, gym time, or been allowed outside since February. Ty was in solitary confinement from February 18, 2017, to March 10, 2017, when he was moved into the general prison population and assaulted. The jail was irresponsible by not placing him in their disabilities unit. That unit was full. For this, we hold the jail accountable. Ty still has blurry vision from the concussion he received and still no MRI. He's still hearing voices. He's being denied an education—this would have been his senior year. We attended his friend's graduation. It took all the strength we could muster.

County Mental Health (CMH) denied him a supervised locked-in-at-night placement in a group home. Now we've found out he has co-morbid illnesses—autism and mental illness. CMH was supposed to give us this information. They, of course, never documented our requests. They also didn't record what happened Friday, the day before his arrest. We begged CMH to help us get a civil commitment.

Today, we hired lawyer #4 for Social Security. Sad to say, next week I'll probably hire lawyer #5 to address the Freedom of Information Act and the denial of the video showing Ty being assaulted, and possibly #6 to obtain an education he has been denied by the jail. This is contrary to state laws. For the record, lawyers #2 & #3 are for his legal cases. Lawyer #1 is for his guardianship.

Sometimes memories flood over me in waves. It's so hard to get rid of anything that reminds me of my little boy. He was a really good boy. He took medicine for ADHD. He had no behavior problems in school. Socialization was hard for him. It's hard not to beat ourselves up, especially about the bullying and how long it was before we realized he was sick. What if we had caught it sooner? It came on so fast.

Ty is eighteen. We've hired eight psychiatrists in his life. I miss my son horribly.

I See Change Coming

—CHANNIN HENRY WILLIAMS

Growing up in a small middle-class town in Washington State, I had very little knowledge or understanding about mental illness, our criminal justice system, the homeless, or how these issues were connected. It wasn't until I was an adult, living in the Houston area, that my eyes were opened to the larger problem. It was not until my own personal experience left me with no doubt that the American mental health care system is insufficient. I believe the inadequate and flawed mental health system plays a large part in why our loved ones end up living on the streets or living in our prisons.

Not long ago, I ran into an old friend, Linda, who lives in a high-rise apartment in downtown Houston. We hadn't talked in years. Because the topic of my daughter came up, Linda told me about her mornings and walking her dogs at 5:30 a.m.

Linda talks passionately about the homeless people she chats with. She describes a man who carries a cardboard box that is used for his bed. Many tell Linda about their loved ones, but their stories are incoherent. She makes healthy muffins for them because she doesn't know when they'll get their next meal. It breaks her heart that she can give them walking directions to a hot meal, warm clothes, and a few other services, but nothing for their mental health needs. Many nights she watches, from her window, as the police escort a homeless person away in a police car.

Those strangers, whom society has written off, belong to someone. What if I lose my own daughter to her mental madness? The optimism in me wants to deny that could happen, but the laws and the mental health system I have lived with remind me it's a real possibility. Would my daughter be harmed or feared by those rushing past her? Would there be someone kind enough to smile at her and feed her a muffin? It gives a bit of comfort knowing there are more Lindas out there who value all human life. We don't hear about them because they don't seek recognition.

My daughter Raven is an amazing person whose early childhood was anything but easy. She was removed from her biological family and two foster homes, and was admitted to her first psychiatric hospital before her fourth birthday. She was then placed in my foster home. When the parental rights were terminated, I adopted her. Shortly after, I got married and she was adopted by my husband and we became a family. She brought so much joy to our lives even when things were difficult.

Raven received a bipolar diagnosis before her fourth birthday, but I didn't believe it. We treated her behaviors as symptoms of post traumatic stress disorder, ADHD, obsessive compulsive disorder, and reactive attachment disorder. She went to therapy and family sessions over the years because of the difficulty we had of raising a child with so many problematic behaviors. Even so, Raven was a cheerful child, who wanted to behave and make the people in her life proud of her. Her quirky personality helped her friends overlook her frequent outbursts, but the peers who couldn't understand her, were often unkind. When I saw small improvements in her daily life, I believed one day all the past abuse would be behind us.

When Raven was 12, one single event seemed to "awaken" mental illness. Our life was suddenly spinning out of control. During the next nine months she was hospitalized eight times. She began experiencing deep depression, which led to manic episodes. Her bipolar diagnosis was confirmed but later changed to schizoaffective disorder. It seemed likely that borderline personality disorder would also be added. Each time the doctors changed her medications and sent her home new symptoms appeared. She began expressing delusional thoughts, and her fantasy world was mixed with what was real. When her hallucinations and obsessions became homicidal, we were advised to get her into long-term treatment.

Then came the most perplexing Medicaid law that did nothing but add to the chaos. In my state, Medicaid wouldn't cover long-term treatment for mental illness unless parents gave up guardianship to the state. Caseworkers who specialized in child abuse (CPS/Child Protective Services) would determine my child's medical care. We first turned to a local post-adoption agency for support and funding. When their funding ended, and it was clear my daughter couldn't return home, we had no choice but to give up guardianship.

CPS agreed to keep Raven in the first residential treatment center (RTC). She lived there for a year, but wasn't getting better. CPS recommended that she go to a long-term psychiatric hospital. I was told, "Your daughter's prognosis looks bleak." While it was hard to hear, it was what I needed to keep me grounded. I knew that it was okay for Raven not to achieve all the dreams I had for her. I was proud of her for working hard and not hating me for sending her away.

The state workers disregarded the recommendation of Raven's medical team and sent her to another RTC. This was a deplorable facility that specialized in treating teen girls who'd been in trouble with the law, not psychiatric patients. The treatment of Raven and me was anything but nice. Raven lasted about 16 days before she tried to strangle herself and was sent to an acute psychiatric hospital. My husband and I hired a lawyer. Because Texas didn't have a long-term psychiatric hospital willing to take Raven, the judge granted an interstate compact. In this case, Texas negotiated an agreement making it possible for Raven to receive psychiatric care in Florida. This process would take time, but the judge ordered that Raven was not to return to the RTC. CPS ignored the referral.

Raven was returned to the RTC. Despite my warnings that Raven would crack in that environment, CPS workers did nothing. Besides making my outrage clear, my legal rights to act were gone. Raven did crack about 18 days after being returned. She had a psychotic, manic episode. The RTC staffers refused to call the crisis intervention team to have Raven assessed. They intended to press criminal charges against her and were uninterested in using the Harris County diversion program.

This arrest added more tension as we scrambled to figure out what would happen next. Would Raven go to Florida or would she stay and face criminal charges? Within 72 hours of her arrest, CPS removed my daughter from the juvenile detention center and put her on a plane to Florida. All charges were dropped. She was 13 years old.

With a different kind of treatment and environment, my daughter improved significantly. She faced consequences if she was defiant, but the approach was different for enforcing the rules and consequences. She learned how to calm herself and learned strategic skills for communicating when she was becoming psychotic. She learned how to express herself when the hallucinations were too loud. Through weekly therapy sessions, my husband and I learned new parenting skills to use when she returned. We were given reasonable expectations to help us set appropriate goals for her.

When Raven returned home from Florida, the transition from being institutionalized for almost two years was extremely difficult. CPS offered little support and, in many ways, made things more difficult. At times, it looked like Raven wouldn't survive outside the security of locked doors and 24-hour monitoring. Most of her suicidal attempts were wrapped in psychotic thinking. One day, for example, while she appeared happy, she swallowed a battery and a few trinkets. She thought if her friend was going to kill himself, she didn't need to live either. These kinds of thoughts and behaviors were common on her good days.

As my husband and I began to anticipate the obstacles we'd be facing when Raven turned 18, we decided to move to our weekend cabin in the hill country at the end of Raven's tenth-grade year. Raven was excited about this move. We set up new school accommodations before moving and made plans to slowly transition her medical care.

It didn't take long for the police to know us and, for the most part, they understood the seriousness of Raven's mental condition. One event, which happened several months before my visit with Linda, left me realizing how easy it would be to lose my daughter to her madness.

After five months, when Raven's illness seemed to be in remission, her paranoia became progressively more problematic. When I agreed to a small medication change, I didn't know it would set off another downward spiral and lead us back to CPS.

While an inpatient, Raven's medication changes happened abruptly. Doctors added and subtracted new medications every few weeks while she was withdrawing from her previous therapeutic combination. Meanwhile, they sent her home even when

I expressed my concerns. It was no surprise that, each time she was released from the hospital, she became sicker and more psychotic. I had the first doctor removed from continuing to treat Raven. He told me the therapeutic level of medication wasn't good for her and he wouldn't prescribe it, even though it had kept her home for almost two years. The second doctor wasn't much better. Raven had a total of six hospitalizations in a six month period.

Raven's biological father had contacted her on social media while her life was going relatively well. At first, she expressed no desire to know him, but her interest was suddenly peaked during the downward spiral. She was enrolled in the partial hospital program on the day she decided to leave our house on foot. Because she was acting strangely, I called the police. When the police assessed her, they determined she didn't meet criteria for a commitment, but admitted she didn't sound coherent.

I'll never understand why the police drove Raven 15 minutes to a local restaurant so she could use the internet to contact her biological father. She wanted him to pick her up so she could live with him. She hadn't seen him since she was three years old and CPS had terminated his rights. I was told, because she was 17, I couldn't stop her, regardless of her severe mental illness. Her biological father lived four-and-a-half hours away. He was only thirty minutes away from getting Raven before the hospital administrator, the police in the next county, and I shut down her plans.

Soon we learned she was being commanded by her hallucinations to kill my husband, me, and her pets, but she didn't want to act. The only solution she could think of to protect us was to find a new home. She was committed back to the psychiatric hospital. My daughter could have left with anyone that day and I might have lost her forever.

When the severity of Raven's symptoms became more dangerous for her to live outside a secure living facility, my husband and I made it clear we could no longer bring her home. Her psychologist agreed. During another psychiatric hospital stay, the doctors finally put in a few requests for long-term hospitals to help get her medications working properly. San Antonio State Hospital did an assessment but declined treating her. Cedar Crest Hospital declined because of "aggression," so Raven was sent home. I was not yet willing to call CPS, so we decided to take another chance, hoping the meds would finally be right.

Less than two weeks later, showing signs of being very sick, our daughter started a fire in our cabin. We were able to put the fire out quickly. When police picked her up, it was clear she needed long-term medical care. They didn't even hint about pressing charges. Only the doctor treating her asked if we were going to press charges, suggesting that might be the best way to get her help. Her psychologist didn't agree with the doctor.

That evening, my husband and I went to the hospital to talk to the doctors and to check on Raven. We were shaken by the events of that day, but we weren't angry with her. She'd been medication compliant. When I entered the hospital room, Raven was entertaining herself with peanut butter and a spoon. After we hugged, I saw that she was behaving like a five-year-old. She showed me her neat trick. She could put the spoon and peanut butter on her nose, and giggled because it wouldn't fall off. She seemed oblivious to the events that had just taken place. The next morning, I called CPS and explained why I was unable to bring my daughter home. My heart broke.

In spite of everything, I see hope. I see more people, like Linda, who care. I see more of us telling our stories so we can make a difference. I see social support groups available online to give advice and support. I see a movement of people who are tired of fighting a system that fails us and has no accountability, and tired of finding our loved ones incarcerated or homeless. I see people educating our politicians and trying to make improvements. I see change coming.

I'm excited to play my small part in fighting for one of the most vulnerable groups of people in our population. I share my story because it needs to be heard.

Update: Raven is back in an acute psychiatric hospital and the doctors have yanked the medication combo that keeps her from the behaviors that we can't live with. Again, they claim the medications are not "good for her"—as if being lost in her psychosis leaves her better off. Raven is begging for ECT or brain surgery—anything to prevent her from losing touch with reality. Anything so she can come home. This brings us full circle as we watch her decline. Her prognosis is looking dim. The meds that keep her functioning the best are being denied to her.

THIS IS MY BELOVED GRANDSON AND I FEAR FOR HIS FUTURE

—MAGGIE WILLIS

"I can't live here, Grandma. Thousands of spiders come out of the vent in the bathroom." Just another day with a challenge for me.

I'd tried to put AJ into an apartment nearby to see how he'd handle being a bit on his own. Still, there was the need to go clean and feed him, as these were not things he would do for himself.

AJ had a childhood history of being "different." There were many diagnoses from a very early age—ADHD (Attention Deficit Hyperactivity Disorder), OCD (Obsessive Compulsive Disorder), ODD (Oppositional Defiant Disorder) and 15 other labels. AJ attended a special-needs school, which was the only option at the time and a long commute. A school that held juvenile delinquents and anyone who made the public school teaching difficult, was no solution for someone who spent most of the time in a fetal position under his desk or in the padded room that increased his anxiety.

At 17, AJ entered a private institution, because it was believed it could help him. The trauma he experienced at the hands of staff specialists was brutal and pushed what may have been moderate schizophrenia into extreme illness. He suffered forced medications and blood work while being tied down, a shaved head, straightjackets, and no visitations—things you would see in old horror movies.

When he was 18, a social worker asked me if I would take AJ. She told me to grieve my grandson's death, as the person I once knew was gone forever. After many classes on what to expect, AJ came to live with me in my belief that love could make this better. Of course, I'd take him. It was a privilege—I'd loved him before he was even a twinkle in his young mother's eye.

There was a short honeymoon period when behavior wasn't frightening, but as time went on, it became clear AJ's mind was more tortured than I ever thought possible.

In the first years he lived with me I tried to teach him to cook—he was afraid to even stand by the stove. He refused to shower or change clothes. He wrapped his legs with chains. He rarely spoke. There were many different personalities to deal with. Hopes for a normal life dwindled. While I was driving him one day and had to stop at a light, he insisted I proceed as there was no car crossing our path. That was the day I realized he should never be encouraged to drive. And when demons came and went uncontrollably, there'd be damage to property, thoughts of death, and letters of dying and darkness.

As I grew older, I needed to know if AJ could live on his own with some help. That's where the apartment idea came in. And by the time I moved him to one, I'd found ways to handle the monsters in the walls and the spiders in the vents. After all, why couldn't there be a special spray that would kill monsters and spiders forever?

I couldn't find solutions for everything, though, and eventually AJ returned to live with me. The days were never normal. A few minutes at a time were okay, but I couldn't leave him alone for more than an hour or two. I lived through painful moments trying to decide if it was time for a 5150 (72-hour involuntary hold) knowing that he would be triaged out as he answered the all-important question: "Are you a danger to yourself or others?" Everyone in the triage area knew how to answer that. There were a few times when a 5150 held and became a 5250 or longer stay, but medications always included terrible side effects.

For AJ, days and nights exist when his tortured mind begs for someone to end his misery. He spends hours telling me he doesn't want to be a burden, even though I try to reassure him I'll always be there for him. And sometimes he warns me to leave the house until his violent thoughts can calm down.

For me, I fill many nights with tears knowing about my grandson's tormented brain. And there's pain, much pain from family and friends who advise, "Put him in an institution or make him homeless." For years, I've tried to educate these people that there are no institutions for him; no homes that can house his extreme condition. Now I ask them to give me a phone number to call, knowing there is no phone number to call. I watch the expressions on their faces, because this is not the reaction they were expecting. They were expecting me to agree and say, "Yes, I'll put him in an institution." There are no appropriate facilities and I know they won't try to help me find one.

Until you experience the disease, until it affects you and you've come to grips with the lack of care and resources available, until you're scared enough to do the research, you're ignorant of the situation. I wonder why others don't thank caregivers for keeping the rest of the family, neighbors, and world safe by watching over and caring for these extremely ill people?

This is my beloved grandson. My heart embraces him. I'm committed to be there for him as long as I'm able to care for him. And I fear for his future when that day ends.

Our Son's
Preventable Death

—PAT WOOD

On March 22, 2019, our son Brian took his own life. My husband and I believe that Brian's suicide could have been prevented if the first group of medical responders and sheriff's officers, whom we called, had acted appropriately.

What follows is a reconstruction of events to the best of our recollection, and a question as to why officers who responded to our 911 call didn't exercise their authority to use an Emergency Custody Order (An ECO allows a person to be taken to a hospital against their will in Virginia) to assist our son, who didn't have the clarity of thought to act in his own interest.

As Brian became increasingly delusional and paranoid over a period of months, he called the Loudoun sheriff non-emergency number several times. Brian had called them when he lived in an apartment in Leesburg and continued to do so when he moved to our house in Sterling. Officers had come to our house in Sterling to investigate imagined break-ins and "suspicious people" loitering around the house several times in the few weeks prior to Brian's suicide.

A deputy responded to these calls and became acquainted with Brian and his mental health status. Because Brian didn't present himself as being a danger to himself or others during these calls, the deputy told us, "I can't take Brian in for a mental health evaluation." We agreed with him at that time.

The last time Brian asked officers to come to the house, this same deputy suggested that we try to get an ECO ourselves from the magistrate on the grounds of "inability to care for self." Please note, Brian had been hospitalized in Loudoun County several times over a seven-year period and had a history of being taken in by the sheriff's office through ECOs issued on our behalf by the magistrate. He'd also been taken for mental health evaluations several times directly by the sheriff's officers because of complaints by neighbors—in one case, because of a domestic assault.

We'd asked, many times, for the Loudoun County Community Service Board to give Brian Assisted Outpatient Treatment (AOT). They always refused. The basis of their refusal was that Brian had private insurance, which we were able to obtain for him through his father's job with the State Department, and because he'd become ill before the age of 22.

On March 22, we were occupied most of the day in supervising the upgrading of our home security system. Because of Brian's paranoia, we thought it might help him feel more secure if we activated an old security system that already existed in the house when we purchased it. We had a technician from the security company in our house from 11:30 a.m. until 5:00 p.m.

We were aware that our son wasn't feeling well and had been vomiting, but we didn't really start paying attention to his condition until after the technician left. Our son had locked himself into an upstairs bathroom and had the water turned on. We assume he hoped the sound of water would camouflage the sound of vomiting. We were able to open the door with a screw driver and found our son crouched on the bathroom floor vomiting into the toilet. His eyes were glazed, and he could barely stand up to walk to the adjoining bedroom. He continued to vomit into a bucket as he sat on the bed.

When we saw his condition, we thought he'd perhaps taken a street drug or overdosed on one of his psychiatric medications. We asked him and he denied it. He said, "I have food poisoning. I'll be fine." We could tell it wasn't food poisoning. Brian's voice was high pitched and abnormal, and his eyes and the ability to walk weren't normal. His vomit was black and looked as though it had blood in it.

We decided to call 911. When the responders to our 911 call arrived, it must have been about 5:45–6:00 p.m. Two sheriff's officers accompanied the medical responders. Our recollection is that there were three or four medical responders. We learned from one of the sheriff's officers that the deputy we knew was not available because he was sick that night. We were upstairs with my son so we didn't see what kind of vehicle the medical responders arrived in. We don't know if it was an ambulance or fire truck.

An older man seemed to be in charge of the medical personnel. He asked my son if he could take his vital signs and my son refused. He asked if they could take him to the emergency room and my son refused. The two sheriff's officers noted to each other that my son had a red mark on his neck where he'd pulled off a chain that he always wore. The older medical person informed us that he could do nothing since my son was refusing treatment. He told me, "Try to persuade your son to be hospitalized." I was also unsuccessful.

It was clear to me that my son was very ill and delusional. I don't believe that the medical people ever examined the contents of the bucket in which my son continued to vomit in their presence. Shortly thereafter, they all left. They were probably in the house about 15 minutes total.

To us, at least, it was obvious that Brian wasn't in a mental state where he could make an informed decision about his own health. He was beyond understanding what anyone was saying to him or urging him to do. The question of whether he had taken some self-harming drug was never addressed. The officers certainly must have been aware of his mental health record from past visits. The red mark on his neck that indicated self-harming behavior was ignored.

We know that police and sheriff's officers are trained to take people in distress into custody and we can't understand why this was not, at least, considered. We pleaded with them, "Please take Brian to a hospital for medical treatment." They didn't exercise their authority to issue an ECO. With hindsight, we think our son was already well along the road to endeavoring to end his life.

Our questions are:

- Did the officers not understand their authority to act in a crisis?
- Had the officers completed the training that is required for this type of situation?
- Did they consider one or more of the three criteria (danger to self, danger to others, inability to care for self) that allows them to act without the consent of an adult?

After the medical responders and the officers left, my husband and I debated about what to do. My husband left the house about 6:30 p.m. to go to the magistrate in Leesburg to try to obtain an ECO. While my husband raced to Leesburg, my son stumbled down the stairs into our office where I was sitting. He sat down and, a few minutes later, had a convulsion. His body went rigid and his eyes rolled back. He'd never had a convulsion before.

I grabbed my cell phone and called 911 again. My son walked into the living room and fell onto the living room couch continuing to vomit into a bucket. He had another massive convulsion. He ended up with his head on the living room floor and his feet pointed at the ceiling. He had no control over his body. When he was able to sit up again. I was still on the phone with 911. I saw a knife poking out from one of his pants pockets. I asked him, "What is that knife was for?"

Brian started having another convulsion. As his arms and body began to get rigid again, he pulled the knife out of his pocket and slit his throat. I told the 911 person what had happened and begged her to get someone to the house quickly. She told me, "Get towels to try to compress the wound on his throat." I ran to the kitchen to get towels but my son pushed me away when I returned to him. Running back to get more towels, I turned around and found Brian standing in the kitchen looking through the trash can. I can only guess that he was looking for the knife.

The 911 lady asked me, "Are there any weapons in the house?" I replied, "No, only kitchen knives." When I said that, my son's attention went to the drawer where we keep the kitchen knives and he started moving toward it. This whole time he was bleeding profusely from the wound in his neck.

I stood in front of the drawer. Brian was getting weak and couldn't push me aside. An officer burst through the kitchen door from the garage and started wrestling with my son, trying to handcuff him. My son struggled against being handcuffed and asked the officer, "Why are you doing this?" The officer saw the blood pouring from the gaping wound on my son's neck. He replied, "I'm trying to save your life."

After several minutes, the officer was able to handcuff Brian. He threw him down on the dining room floor. At that point, medical personnel came into the house. It was too late, since my son had lost so much blood. Medical personnel worked on him for thirty minutes with no success. We believe he died on the dining room floor.

Brian was taken to Reston Hospital in an ambulance. My husband arrived back from Leesburg, and we rushed to the hospital where we sat in a waiting room for 45 minutes. A doctor came out and told us, "We weren't able to save Brian. He lost too much blood and we weren't able to get a heartbeat."

We so wish that the first call to 911 had resulted in getting my son medical treatment and then mental health treatment. The medical examiner's office stated on the death certificate that the "Immediate cause of death is pending." We've asked for, but haven't received, the results of any toxicology screening. With the constant vomiting and the convulsions, it's possible that some drug or overdose of medication was involved.

We hope, in the future, the mental health of the ill person and his/her ability to make informed and rational decisions be taken into consideration by medical responders, and that they defer to sheriff's officers regarding a possible ECO. The possibility of an attempt at suicide must also be taken into serious account when deciding whether or not to leave the scene. An opportunity to save my son's life was missed and resulted, in our opinion, in a tragedy that could have been avoided. Our family is devastated by Brian's loss. He was 38 years old.

We hope our story will prevent this kind of heartbreaking outcome for another family.

Conclusion

The Close

So you're done. You've finished reading our stories. Thank you for your attention.

I hope, we hope, that our stories will make a difference. That they'll reap more public understanding about serious mental illness (SMI). That they'll generate political will to take action, and begin the arduous process of building anew America's mental health system.

We're not naive. We've lived through too much to be naive. The complexities involved in mental healthcare reform are daunting. We know things cannot be fixed overnight. But we have to start. Nothing will be fixed if we don't start.

To start, SMI has to be recognized and acknowledged. For centuries SMI has been lost, consistently, to other events of the day. Just like today—pandemics, climate concerns, political upheaval, societal unrest, racial tensions, international discord, opioid poisoning, income disparities, poverty, food insecurity, immigration, homelessness, and violence—and every other dilemma on the planet—take precedence over SMI. Do a Google search of the top ten issues confronting the US right now. Healthcare shows up as a main issue, but if it shows up at all, mental health/illnesscare is mentioned tangentially—as an afterthought. As always, serious mental illness is buried so deep in the proverbial heap that it never beeps on the "we need to take care of this" radar screen. SMI advocates are not trying to minimize other pressing national/global challenges. We simply want to be included. We want SMI assigned meaningful ranking on the list of national problems that must be addressed ASAP.

Please note: Serious mental illness intersects with all the major socio/economic/health problems listed above.

SMI warriors envy the robust LGBTQ and Black Lives Matter campaigns. SMI advocacy is thwarted by the fact that affected individuals are often too ill to fight for themselves; and many times, family stress levels exceed family coping capacity. As Linda Rippee Privatte—one of the writers in this book—says, "Families are the collateral damage of our mental health system."

There is a theory out there referenced as "structural violence." It alludes to deep-rooted ways social constructs (like our current mental health system) can harm or disadvantage individuals. In this theory, usually, no specific person can or will be held responsible to dismantle and reform the debasing system.

I'm reminded of this story:

This is a story about four people named Everybody, Somebody, Anybody, and Nobody. There was an important job to be done and Everybody was sure that Somebody would do it. Anybody could have done it, but Nobody did. Somebody got angry because it was Everybody's job. Everybody thought Anybody could do it, but Nobody realized that Everybody wouldn't do it. It ended up that Everybody blamed Somebody when Nobody did what Anybody could have.

A tad convoluted, but you get the drift. The bottom line is no one took responsibility so nothing got accomplished. Similarly, *nobody* is being held responsible to improve our mental health system even though it's *everybody's* job. Sure, multiple pockets of forward action exist. But a coordinated government effort with national implementation plans? With "the buck stops here" authority? Haven't heard of one.

So what can I do? What can you do? In the next few pages, I've included a Grassroots Five-Part Plan to Address Serious Mental Illness and a sample cover letter. In 2019 I quarterbacked this plan which was collaboratively developed by SMI advocates from across the country. It's a starting point. We're asking Everybody, Somebody, and Anybody (sorry Nobody) to share this plan with their political representatives, doctors, therapists, psychiatrists, pastors, families, neighbors, and friends. That's one thing each of us can do.

I've also added a list—right after this section—of twenty-five actions each of us could take. If each of us takes one or two of the suggested actions, we'll intensify the call for better mental health/ illness care and a Department of Actually Doing Something.

As it stands today, the US mental health/illness system is filled with political landmines and gut-wrenching divisions: parents vs. children, peer organizations vs.family organizations, voluntary vs. involuntary treatment concepts, psychiatrist vs. psychologist turf wars, state vs. federal jurisdictions, HIPAA restrictions vs parental rights, lack of beds vs. incarceration, unions vs. providers, psychiatry vs. anti-psychiatry, civil rights vs. dying with your rights on, NIMBYism vs. housing, traditional medicine vs. holistic medicine, and funded advocacy organizations vs. unfunded grassroots advocacy efforts. I watched my son Pat die because the system is tied up in bureaucratic and philosophical knots.

Your reading *Tomorrow Was Yesterday,* and considering what you can do to help our SMI families, is appreciated by SMI mothers/caregivers writing in this book and by SMI mothers/caregivers everywhere. "Thank you" is an understatement. We value your alliance more than you will ever know.

—DEDE RANAHAN
July 23, 2020

YOUR
CHOICES

1. Open your mind.
2. Open your heart.
3. Talk about serious mental illness (SMI).
4. Educate yourself about SMI.
5. Review your family history—substance abuse, suicide, depression—and watch for signs of SMI in your children or other family members. Get help early.
6. If you're a caregiver, take care of yourself, too.
7. Reach out to your family/friends/neighbors who struggle with SMI and acknowledge their pain. Ask what you can do for them.
8. Be political. Send a copy of the *Grassroots Five-Part Plan to Address SMI* to your local, state, and federal representatives.
9. Elect political leaders who will establish a national mental health/mental illness program with national implementation plans.
10. Go to school—or back to school—and become a social worker, a psychologist, a psychiatrist, a nurse-practitioner,

a counselor, a judge, or an attorney specializing in SMI cases.

11. Push for clean, warm, welcoming supported housing. You know, NIMBY kind of housing.
12. Allow NIMBY housing in your own backyard.
13. Become a pen pal with an SMI prisoner—in solitary or out of solitary.
14. Join SMI advocacy groups and organizations.
15. Share your SMI stories at www.soonerthantomorrow.com.
16. Find support groups in your area to help yourself. Or start a support group.
17. Promote laws/actions that reclassify SMI as a neurological brain disorder.
18. Back laws/actions that reform HIPAA (Health Insurance Portability and Accountability Act.)
19. Support laws/actions that repeal Medicaid's Institutes for Mental Disease (IMD) Exclusion.
20. Lobby for programs that provide a full continuum of care.
21. Fight for the decriminalization of SMI.
22. When seeking help for yourself or a loved one, push through biases and flaws in the mental health system. Persist.
23. See the big picture. Make sure other social woes aren't allowed to obscure SMI needs.
24. Celebrate small/all SMI victories.
25. Say "No" to promises of change tomorrow. Tomorrow was yesterday.

A Grassroots Five-Part Plan to Address Serious Mental Illness (SMI)

*This plan was developed collaboratively in 2019
by SMI advocates from across the country.*

1. **Reclassify Serious Mental Illness (SMI)** From a Behavioral Condition to What It Is, a Neurological Medical Condition.

   Why Reclassification is Important

   Reclassification will unlock more research funding and help eliminate discrimination in treatment, insurance reimbursement, and the perception of SMI as "behavioral" condition. SMI is a human rights issue. NIMH ranks SMI among the top 15 causes of disability worldwide, with an average lifespan reduction of 28 years.

   Presidential Action
   - Create a cabinet position exclusively focused on SMI.
   - Push for congressional appropriations to include schizophrenia in a CDC program that collects data

on the prevalence and risk factors of neurological conditions in the US population.

2. Reform The Health Insurance Portability and Accountability Act (HIPAA)

Why HIPAA Reform Is Important
Overly strict HIPAA laws make it extremely difficult for families and caregivers to partner in the treatment of their loved ones, resulting in important life-saving medical information gaps. By eliminating this barrier, family support will be strengthened, reducing the chance of relapse, homelessness, imprisonment, and death.

Presidential Action
- Work with legislators to change HIPAA law to ensure mental health professionals are legally permitted to share and receive critical diagnostic criteria and treatment information with/from parents or caregivers of SMI.

3. Repeal Medicaid's Institutes for Mental Disease (IMD) Exclusion

Why IMD Repeal Is Important
IMD repeal will increase the availability of psychiatric inpatient beds. The IMD exclusion is not only discriminatory to those suffering from neurological brain disorders, it is a leading cause of our national psychiatric hospital bed shortage. It prohibits Medicaid payments to states for those receiving psychiatric care in a facility with more than 16 beds who are 21–65, the age group with the most SMI.

Presidential Action
- Work with legislators to repeal the IMD exclusion.

4. Provide a Full Continuum of Care

Why a Full Continuum of Care Is Important
A continuum of care insures that SMI patients receive early intervention at all stages of their illnesses, long-term care when needed, and follow-up treatment (medications and therapies) when they're released. It reduces visits to jails, ERs, and hospitals, homelessness, and morgues. A continuum of care provides lifetime management.

Presidential Action
- Create federal incentives for states to address a full array of inpatient, outpatient, and supportive housing care.

5. Decriminalize Serious Mental Illness (SMI)

Why Decriminalization of SMI Is Important
People suffering with other neurological conditions, like Alzheimer's and dementia, can get treatment promptly without being kicked out of their homes to wander the streets until they are arrested and put in jail or prison rather than a hospital. Serious mental illness is the only disease where the doors to treatment are shut unless a crime is committed. This is pure and simple discrimination, with the disastrous results we see in our country today—homelessness, incarceration, the disintegration of families, and death.

Presidential Action
- Work with legislators and others to change "must be a danger to self or others" criteria.
- Work with legislators and others to change involuntary commitment criteria and redefine it in objective terms based on scientific medical need for treatment. Psychosis, like a stroke, is a traumatic brain injury and needs immediate treatment for the best outcome.

An Extended List of SMI Needs

*This list was developed collaboratively in 2019
by SMI advocates from across the country.*

1. **Reclassify Serious Mental Illness (SMI)** From a Behavioral Condition to What It Is—a Neurological Medical Condition

2. **Reform The Health Insurance Portability and Accountability Act (HIPAA)**
   - Present patients and families with a social worker to support the family unit throughout the care process, including medication and psychiatric treatment.
   - Require mandatory HIPAA training for everyone in the medical profession and mandate a test on proven knowledge.
   - Develop a federal program for the administration of psychiatric advance directives (PAD), which include a universal release of information and designate an agent if a patient's capacity is lost.

3. Repeal Medicaid's Institutes for Mental Disease (IMD) Exclusion

4. Provide a Full Continuum of Care
   - Provide inpatient care (IMD waivers), outpatient care (i.e., AOT, Clubhouses), and a full array of housing (locked stabilization to unlocked intensive, medium intensive, and peer-run.).
   - Require a psychiatric standard of care for various SMI diagnoses, as with other medical specialties.
   - Require prescriptions based on need not ROI for the insurance industry
   - Remove ERs as entry for mental illness hospitalization. The ER process and its chaotic environment aren't conducive to the well-being of SMI patients.

5. Decriminalize Serious Mental Illness
   - Eliminate solitary confinement in jails and prisons.
   - Support nationwide civil mental health courts and expand criminal ones that are already established to keep those suffering from SMI out of jails and prisons.
   - Establish mental health courts on a federal level, and coordinate federal courts and state-run mental illness facilities.
   - Move crimes committed by SMI sufferers adjudicated in the federal system into state courts.
   - Mandate a way for families to provide medical history to jail/prison doctors to inform treatment.
   - Fund a digitized system for medical records in counties/hospitals to jails so information can be transferred immediately upon arrest and incarceration.
   - Provide uniform psychiatric screening of the incarcerated.

- Use standardized protocols for medication of SMI prisoners.
- Require strict limits on delays for trial time.

6. **Pay Attention to Supportive Housing**
   - Provide 24/7 supervised housing for those who cannot live independently.
   - Provide defined levels of support built around a person's needs, especially long-term care.
   - Clarify Olmstead for SMI. Least restrictive care isn't always least expensive or best.
   - Examine, don't ignore, a person's ability to handle and benefit from a less restrictive setting.

7. **Revamp Involuntary Treatment**
   - Use lack of insight (anosognosia) as one of the criteria for determining involuntary treatment.
   - Establish a federal standardized "need for treatment" involuntary commitment law.
   - Base restrictive settings on actual abilities, not wishful thinking or one-track plans.

8. **Include Education**
   - Require mandatory, institutionalized education about SMI for judges, sheriffs, attorneys, district attorneys, law enforcement, and first responders.
   - Require units of SMI education for educators—preschool through university.
   - Improve Crisis Intervention Training and expand training to all counties.
   - Provide a health proxy form for college students to allow them to release medical information and name who can take care of them in a crisis.

- Hold universities accountable and required to connect students to crisis intervention, especially during medical leave.

9. Give Incentives
   - Incentivize the expansion of medical schools to graduate more psychiatrists, child psychiatrists, internists with psychiatry specialties, psychiatric nurse practitioners, and physician assistants.
   - Allow loan forgiveness for providers treating SMI patients.
   - Give incentives for rural psychiatrists.
   - Incentivize more long-term treatment/stabilization of individuals with SMI.
   - Give incentives to psychiatrists to accept health insurance, especially Medicaid.

10. Expand Assisted Outpatient Treatment (AOT)
    - Federally clarify AOT and create a federal model for AOT law.
    - Offer AOT immediately to everyone upon diagnosis.

11. Improve Hospitals
    - Build regional federal hospitals for patients who cannot be treated in their home state's hospitals because of lack of beds.
    - Improve reimbursements to hospitals which lose revenue on SMI patients.
    - End hospital discrimination against SMI "violent" patients and those "difficult to discharge."

12. **Increase Research and Epidemiology**
    - Fund NIMH research specifically for SMI.
    - Establish a Disability Advocacy Program for legal services for SMI when counties/states fail to provide long-term support services or when insurance/managed care and Medicaid fail to cover/pay for long-term supported services and treatment.
    - Pursue better national epidemiology studies for people with SMI.
    - Establish a federal law that requires states to track each SMI diagnosis with bad outcomes like death, homelessness, and incarceration.

13. **Revisit Parity**
    - Clarify parity for SMI and include Medicaid and Medicare in parity law.
    - Enforce violations against parity law.

14. **Address Social Security and Disability Income Issues**
    - Change the way Social Security income for the disabled is taken by states when a patient is admitted to state operated mental health institutions, residential care facilities, and hospitals.
    - Increase disability income to a level where a person can survive and maintain reasonable housing.

15. **Create Psychiatric Campuses**
    - Build psychiatric campuses with multiple levels of care, supportive housing from most restrictive to least restrictive, and separate independent living apartments.

- Provide on-campus coffee shops, gyms, recreational facilities, and gardens where people with SMI could work with support as needed.
- Provide substance abuse treatment services, AA, or NA meetings.

Sample Cover Letter

To: All Federal, State, and Local Political Candidates

Subject: Serious Mental Illness (SMI)

So far, political candidates make rare mention of serious mental illness (SMI—schizophrenia, schizo-affective disorder, OCD, bipolar disorder, and major depression), and the lack of mental health/illness care in the US.

- The SMI population represents 4–5 percent (11 million) of the mentally ill in the US. That's 11 million families and extended families (voters).
- Ten times as many people with SMI are incarcerated as are hospitalized.
- Some SMI individuals are so sick they don't realize they're sick (anosognosia), don't respond to treatment (if they get it) and end up incarcerated, homeless, missing, suicidal or dead.
- It will cost billions to create a viable mental illness system. The cost of *not caring* is costing billions, now, in prison overpopulation, homelessness, cities under siege, lost workdays, family disintegration, suicides, untimely

deaths, inundated ERs and hospitals, violence caused by untreated SMI, overwhelmed police, and in uninformed and misinformed criminal justice systems.

The Grassroots Five-Part Plan enclosed is the collaborative work of advocates from across the country—individuals, professionals, writers, journalists, caregivers, and mothers (always the mothers). Our intent is to put this plan in front of candidates in forthcoming political cycles.

The steps in our plan are baby steps. We can't immediately address everything that needs to be addressed in our nonexistent mental illness system, but we have to start somewhere. We're trying to help candidates—we know you have a lot on your plates and we appreciate your energy and efforts to make our country better. We've created this Grassroots Five-Part Plan to give you a starting point and a way to introduce SMI into political discourse and public conversation.

We're asking you to take four initial actions:

1. Please read our plan and make it your own.
2. Put your SMI plan on your campaign website.
3. Talk about SMI on the campaign trail and in campaign debates.
4. Talk with us. We're willing and eager to help you as you move forward.

The SMI community is searching for its political champions. We're a large, passionate, motivated, frustrated, hurting, and determined block of voters. We look forward to hearing from you.

About the Contributors

Theresa A.—"You Don't Matter" & "There's No Limit To What A Mother Will Do"—Theresa has been a preschool teacher for many years. She lives in New Hampshire with her husband. (New Hampshire)

Holly Alston—"Mommy, Please Clear My Name"—Holly's son, Terrell, suffered from schizophrenia and other mental health issues. He was in prison for over seven years while his mental health was ignored. When Terrell was in isolation, he would scrape his eyebrows off and pluck out his eyelashes. "He was released from prison 8/8/16 and by 8/20/16, he was dead." (Pennsylvania)

Margie Annis—"Losing My Child Barbarically"—Margie sees herself as a mother first in what is important in life. She has nothing but unconditional love for her children (sons). The youngest was difficult and different. "We are all learning as we live life to understand it. When this son was a man, the sky fell in, and now he is gone forever. Our love for him will never die." (Alabama)

Anonymous—"I Just Want My Beautiful Boy Back"—"I'm still new at having a son diagnosed with mental illness and with navigating the system for help. Any system requires a herculean effort. I hope and pray for a better future for these who have mental illnesses." (California)

April—"Helping Mr. K"—April is a wife, retired direct marketing creator, and sibling to Mr. K. Her mother died seven years ago with no plan in place for her brother's care other than the designation of "Social Security Payee." (Washington)

Audrey Adams Auernheimer—"For Now I'm Thankful Adam Is Alive"—Audrey is the mother of four children, three of whom have been diagnosed with mental illness. Her son Marty was diagnosed with schizophrenia at age 22. Her only daughter, Candace, was diagnosed with depression with suicidal ideation at age 12. Marty died at 28 and Candace died at 26 by suicide. Her 30-year-old son, also diagnosed, lives with her. The youngest son remains untreated and barely functional, mostly due to anosognosia. (Oklahoma)

Harriet B—"I'm Gonna Brag About My Son"—(Kentucky)

Kathy Baker—"Letters From Solitary Confinement"—(California)

Gwendolyn Bartley—"It's Kind of Like a Daily 'Sophie's Choice'"—Gwendolyn is the mother of five (now adult) children through the blessings of adoption and natural birth. She is the founder and executive director of Amazing Grace Advocacy, a nonprofit that supports families raising children with brain disorders in Concord, North Carolina. Gwendolyn serves on several community, state, and national initiatives to advocate for access to appropriate services for children with serious emotional disturbances (SED). (North Carolina)

Tama Bell—"Nightmares in the Daylight" & "10 Myths Mental Health Officials Tell Us About Our Kids" (New York)

Joyce Berryman—"Stuck in Texas"—(Texas)

Ronni Blumenthal—"No One Asks. She's Been Erased"—Ronnie is a mother, advocate, writer, daughter, and wife. "It won't change unless we talk about it." (Florida)

Judy Waldo Bracken—"Between Now and the Next Full Moon"—Judy is the mother of three sons, a writer, and a swimming coach living in the East Bay, California. In 2010, her husband was diagnosed with stage 4 cancer and her middle son with serious mental illness while a senior in college. The following years were full of cancer treatments, clinical trials, police calls, psych wards and 5150s. Since then, her husband has passed away and her son has been placed under LPS conservatorship. (California)

Mara Briere—"A Problem Shared Is a Problem Halved"—Mara is the mother, aunt, daughter, and sister of adults with serious mental illness. She's a Master's Level Certified Family Life Educator. She's founded a nonprofit for families uprooted by mental illness, Grow a Strong Family, in order to generate, share, and develop the resources, support, and network that families like hers need and do not have. (Massachusetts)

Allison Brown—"Fighting for Change"—Allison is a 37-year-old wife and mother of three. "I want a better life for my kids than I had. I hope to be a voice of change for mental health reform." (Florida)

Kendra Burgos—"The Caregiver's Sadness"—Kendra's hope is that others will know there is love and joy despite the many challenges of living with someone with mental illness. "I am grateful to my husband for teaching me how to love unconditionally, and to my children for their strength, because it is the family's struggle as well." Kendra wants others to know that we are not alone, and there is strength in our stories. (Connecticut)

GG Burns—"Anosognosia—#1 Enemy"—**George Burns** writes: "My late wife, GG Burns, was an incredible advocate for those who suffer from SMI. Gina, as I call her, was a wonderful, loving mother and unbelievable artist—with no boundaries to her creativity. I will always love you, Gina Burns." (Alabama)

Mary A. Butler—"Let's Talk About Hopeful Voluntary Admissions"—(Pennsylvania)

Sarah C—"It Feels Like the State of Michigan Wants Me Dead"—(Michigan)

Leslie Carpenter—"What Do I Dream of Now?"—Leslie is an advocate for people with serious brain disorders in Iowa, along with her husband, Scott. They've advocated on federal policy changes with all the democratic presidential candidates during the 2020 pre-caucus season. Leslie is a board member of NAMI Johnson County and teaches Family-to-Family, NAMI Provider training, and serves on the Advocacy and Outreach

Committee. The Carpenters have two adult children, one of whom lives with schizoaffective disorder. (Iowa)

Sylvia Charters—"There's No Help in the USA"—Sylvia is the mother of two sons. Her son Jason had bipolar disorder with psychosis. He passed at age 40 with cardiomyopathy. Her youngest son is undiagnosed and living, homeless, on the streets of Phoenix and is addicted to street drugs. He has symptoms of bipolar disorder. "There's no help whatsoever for the mentally sick in the USA." (Florida)

Laurie Lethbridge Christmas—"What an Effing Nightmare"— (New York)

Jerri Clark—"My Goal Is Not Happiness but Human Understanding"—Jerri advocates for treatment access in Washington State, where she started Mothers of the Mentally Ill (MOMI). She and her husband (married since 1994) have a daughter and two grandsons. Their son, Calvin, died by suicide March 18, 2019. (Washington)

Dawn MacTaggart Connolly—"What Is the Answer?"—(Iowa)

Elizabeth Courtois—"Helping My Daughter Have a Childhood"— Elizabeth is a 34-year-old single mother of four. She's raising three children at home alone. Her daughter Eva is living in a residential facility. (Wisconsin)

Sonia Fletcher Dinger—"Our Family Tragedy"—Sonia lives in Mount Shasta, California, with her second husband, a dog, a cat, and 15 chickens. She works part-time at a rural hospital and has served on the County Behavioral Health Board. Her daughter Christina is on conditional release from Napa State Hospital. She lives in a group home, has a part-time job, and continues to work hard toward recovery. "I am so proud of her. We speak on the phone almost every day." (California)

Ashley Doonan and Cathie Curtis—"I Am Ashley. I Define Me."—Cathy's daughter Ashley fought a good fight to reduce the stigma associated with mental illness in academia, the workplace, the correctional system, and society as a whole. Cathie writes, "Although she is no longer with us, I am her voice." (New Hampshire)

Donna Erickson—"What I've Learned About Our Broken Mental Health System"—Donna is the mother of a son (age 35) who has a serious brain illness. "As a mental health reform activist, I hope to see much needed major changes for our loved ones. We are long overdue for a better mental health system." (Massachusetts)

Deborah Fabos—"What Are Your Family's Numbers?"—Deborah is the mother and caregiver of an adult son with a neurobiological disorder more commonly known as schizophrenia. She's an advocate for family members/caregivers and those who suffer with the consequences of untreated and treatment resistant anosognosia (lack of insight into their condition). Deborah created a Facebook support page and has been its administrator for six years. "I passionately support the reclassification of schizophrenia under neurology." (California)

Heidi Franke—"I Am Livid, Shaking"—Heidi is an RN. She's been living through the diagnosis of her youngest son's pervasive mental illness and struggles with addiction. Her goal is to empower parents to speak up to help overcome obstacles to care for their children. "By telling our stories, we give permission to others to start telling theirs." Heidi makes mending herself a personal daily engagement project "as we must put on our oxygen mask first to help those beside us." (Utah)

Julia Gillies—"This Is Exhausting"—"I've been a mental health advocate in New Jersey for 11 years. I read. I research. I witness the suffering of those with mental illness as a loving mother. I send emails, texts, and letters, and make phone calls. Yet, my cries for help often go unheard. Change doesn't happen until action occurs to help those suffering with SMI. We must wake up, educate others, and be persistent." (New Jersey)

Jeanne Gore—"We Need a Revolution"—Jeanne is a family member and coordinator and co-chair of the Steering Committee for the National Shattering Silence Coalition (NSSC). (Maine)

Val Greenoak—"Jesse and Me"—Val is the mother of five. Jesse was her fourth son. All her children are grown. "I live quietly on a couple of acres in the redwoods." (California)

Deborah Harper—"I Feared He'd Be Blown to Pieces"—Deborah is a teacher, mother, and friend. She is a designer and photographer. She is a Christian/Catholic. (Massachusetts)

CJ Hanson—"Beyond My Understanding of What Being Human Means"—Catherine J. Rippee-Hanson is Linda Rippee Privatte's twin sister and Mark Hanson's sister. They've been seeking help and services for Mark for 33 years. "It's not gotten any easier. I can no longer go out looking for him and have to rely on Linda's accounts of losing and finding him over and over again. Local, regional, state, and federal laws impede our path every step of the way." (California)

Amy Kerr—"I Feel Incredibly Blessed"—(Maryland)

Nikki Landis—"Nikki and Kevin"—Nikki is the mother of five and homeschools her children on a small farm in rural Ohio. She loves to read and learn new perspectives. Her childhood dream was to have a large family, live in the country, and write. She continues to pursue her dreams despite how SMI has affected her life, and she encourages everyone to do the same. (Ohio)

Martha—"Everyone Needs Hope"—Martha is the proud mother to her son who lives heroically with SMI (or neurological brain disorder). Along with advocacy and prayer, "I long for the day when our loved ones who are suffering will have the opportunity to receive effective, compassionate care like all others." (Kentucky)

Carole McAfee—"A Mother's Fight"—(Oregon)

Angela McCandless—"We Don't Help People Here"—Angela is mother to four children and grandma to four children. She writes: "Here are four words to describe me: 1. Organized—organize don't agonize. 2. Determined—I'll never give up fighting for my son. 3. Spiritual—I don't believe in miracles—I rely on them. 4. Kind—I love making someone's day. My hobbies are decorating and cooking. A favorite quote: 'If you are on the right path, it will always be uphill.'" (Idaho)

Sherri McGimsey—"What Would You Do?"—Sherri is a wife, mother of two sons, grandmother, business owner for 39 years, and a national advocate for SMI. Her eldest son, Matt, has schizophrenia. Sherri's a member of NAMI South Mountains, North Carolina, and serves on the NSSC (Nation Shattering Silence Coalition.) She's a trainer in NAMI's Family-to-Family class and in the Crisis Intervention Team (CIT) for police and law enforcement. "A Mother's Prayer for Mental Illness" guides her on this journey. (North Carolina)

Jacque Cowger McKinney—"Too Many Families Live This Pain"—(Illinois)

Rhonda Meth—"We Received the Worst Call of Our Lives"— Rhonda is more of a spiritual person than religious. She's grateful for her husband, daughters Monica and Amanda, and her family and good friends. Usually, she's a calm person and strong mentally. She enjoys yoga, reading books, and painting. "The loss of our Monica was devastating. It left a hole in our hearts that will never be filled." (California)

Kelli Nidey—"Have You Seen My Son?"—Kelli lives in a little river town in the Midwest. "I hope we can find causes and cures for neurological illnesses in my lifetime." (Indiana)

Teresa Pasquini—"Teresa and Danny"—Teresa advocates for reforming the nation's mental health system. With a son and brother living with SMI, her 45-year personal experience drives her passion. She's provided testimony in forums, including the Institute of Healthcare Improvement, the National Quality Forum, and an event on Capitol Hill advocating for "The Helping Families in Mental Health

Crisis Act." The Bay Area Newsgroup recognized Teresa for her local advocacy during 2017's Women's History Month. (California)

Laura Pogliano—"Zac, My Darling Son" & "Let's Talk About Real Issues"—Laura is a training and education consultant in Baltimore, Maryland. She lost her only son, Zaccaria, to schizophrenia in 2015. Laura is a former board member of SARDAA (Schizophrenia and Related Disorders Alliance of America), and leads the Maryland SARDAA State chapter, which advocates for reform and the reclassification of schizophrenia to neurology. (Maryland)

Linda Rippee Privatte—"Rewind and Erase"—Linda advocates, along with her twin sister, CJ Hanson, for their traumatic brain injured, blind, SMI, homeless brother. She seeks legislative changes that would allow him to receive treatment for the brain disease that is his serious mental illness. "The mental health system has collapsed on the backs of the families of SMI loved ones, while tying their hands legally." (California)

Dede Ranahan—"Looking For Joy"—Dede is the editor of *Tomorrow Was Yesterday* and the author of *Sooner Than Tomorrow—A Mother's Diary About Mental Illness, Family, and Everyday Life*. She dedicates her mental illness advocacy to her son, Patrick (1968–2014). She has three daughters and six grandchildren. "I love them lots." (California)

Rebecca Reinig—"I'm Prepared for Joey's Death"—"I am a mother, advocate for my son, pacifist, and trying to be one of the voices for those who cannot speak for themselves." (California)

Karen Riches—"Our Pledge"—"I'm a mom. My son meant the world to me. Jacob suffered with serious mental illness. He was diagnosed with schizophrenia. Too bad that my son meant nothing to the medical community. He died because of their beliefs and lack of knowledge about mental illness."(New York)

Ellie Shukert—"Dorothea Dix Reborn"—Elllie volunteered during the 1960s at the Worcester State Hospital in Massachusetts. It was established in 1830 and expanded during the 1840s, largely through the efforts of Dorothea Dix. This hospital, now Worcester Recovery, still serves SMI patients in a modern facility. Dorothea had a "breakdown" herself and was cared for in England by a practitioner of "moral treatment." She wanted others to have a chance to become well again. "That lady ran right over stigma." (California)

Kat Shultz—"A Mother's Request in Court"—Kat is the 51-year-old mother of five children. Her eldest child passed away in 2013. She's been a teacher since 1991 and currently teaches fourth grade. (California)

Kecia Bolken Speck—"I'm Never Calling the Crisis Team or the Police Again"—Kecia is the mother of two adult children and currently lives in rural Oregon. She works in pediatric occupational therapy and takes care of her 29-year-old son full-time. Her dreams for the future are to change the education of first responders, to ensure the funding of skilled crisis teams, and to decriminalize serious mental illness. "My family's lives depend on it. Nobody should ever have to go through this alone." (Oregon)

Joann Strunk—"Finding Sarah"—Joann is the mother of a smart, beautiful young woman of 33 who has been seriously mentally ill since age 16. "The battle to get her the care that she needs has been horrendous. Our mental health system is beyond broken." (Kentucky)

Laurie Turley—"They Should Have Let You Help Me. I Wasn't In My Right Mind."—Laurie is a musician, music teacher, wife, mother, grandmother and advocate of "treatment before tragedy." (Maine)

Sandy Turner—"He Has Schizophrenia, Your Honor"—(Florida)

Sharon Underwood—"Why Is This Okay?"—Sharon is a single mother of four. Her mentally ill son, Tim, is her youngest child. Sharon's been a caregiver for the elderly for over 25 years. (Oregon)

Cheri VanSant—"We Need Holistic Healthcare for People With SMI"—Cheri is a 65-year-old retired RN and the mother of a 43-year-old son with serious mental illness. She used to teach NAMI's Family-to-Family classes and advocated for family members and those who struggle with the illness. As a healthcare professional at the time of her story, "I was unaware of how dismissive doctors and nurses were to my dear friend's illness and was curious how often this occurs." (Arizona)

Francie VanZandt—"Prepare Myself? How Do I Do That?"— Francie is 62 years old and the mother of five children. She's spent many years working at the elementary school in her rural community. "I am a strong woman. Life has not been easy. Like all of us, a few tough times have come my way. Some of those times I didn't think I could survive. I did. I manage to begin each new day with the hope I can make a difference for someone." (California)

Darlene Been Watkins—"Please Don't Kill My Son"—(Colorado)

Christi Weeks—"Please Help Find Ryan"—(Arizona)

Kimberlee Cooper West—"Walk a Mile in Our Shoes"—(Michigan)

Channin Henry Williams—"I See Change Coming"—After 14 years of giving so much of herself to meet her daughter's special needs, Channin is now focusing on her husband, hobbies, and finding her way. "Raven left the institution on her 18th birthday. Soon, all communication stopped. My greatest nightmare came true. How should a mother like me grieve or even feel? It is my supportive family and faith in Jesus Christ that has given me strength and hope that change is coming." (Texas)

Maggie Willis—"This Is My Beloved Grandson and I Fear for His Future"—Maggie was raised in Santa Clara's Silicon Valley in the '50s and '60s. She became a mother, grandmother, and great-grandmother. "My first grandchild helped me understand that people do not consider brain problems the same as other medical problems; and the caretaker not only suffers from watching their loved one suffer from a tortured brain, but from the ignorance of friends and family." (California)

Pat Wood—"Our Son's Preventable Death"—After his first year of college, Pat's elder son was diagnosed with bipolar disorder. "His death by suicide at age 38 was the outcome we'd fought against for years and was our worst nightmare come true." Pat's younger son also has a mental illness. "There have been many medications, hospitals, therapists, psychiatrists, and less-than-successful battles to get the services my children needed. My younger son's uncertain future remains my concern and focus now." (Virginia)

GLOSSARY

AA—Alcoholics Anonymous is an international fellowship with the stated purpose of enabling its members to stay sober and to help other alcoholics achieve sobriety.

ACT Program—Assertive Community Treatment is a team-based model that provides intensive mental health services and supports to people with serious mental health/substance abuse issues.

ADA—The Americans with Disabilities Act became law in 1990.

ADHD—Attention deficit hyperactivity disorder is a mental health disorder that can cause above-normal levels of hyperactive and impulsive behaviors.

Alzheimer's—A progressive disorder that causes brain cells to waste away and die. Alzheimer's disease is the most common cause of dementia—a continuous decline in thinking, and in behavioral and social skills that disrupts a person's ability to function independently.

Anorexia—An eating disorder characterized by weight loss (or lack of appropriate weight gain in growing children); difficulties maintaining an appropriate body weight for height, age, and stature; and, in many individuals, distorted body image.

Anosognosia—A deficit of self-awareness, a condition in which a person with a disability is unaware of having it.

Baker Act—The Florida Mental Health Act of 1971 allows the involuntary institutionalization and examination of an individual.

Bipolar Disorder—A mental disorder that causes unusual shifts in mood, energy, activity levels, concentration, and the ability to carry out day-to-day tasks.

Bipolar 1 Disorder—Is defined by manic episodes that last at least seven days, or by manic symptoms that are so severe that the person needs immediate hospital care.

Bipolar 2 Disorder—Is defined by a pattern of depressive episodes and hypomanic episodes, but not the full-blown manic episodes that are typical of Bipolar I Disorder.

CDC—Centers for Disease Control and Prevention is dedicated to protecting health and promoting quality of life through prevention and control of disease, injury, and disability.

Childhood Onset Schizophrenia—Is essentially the same as schizophrenia in adults, but it occurs early in life and has a profound impact on a child's behavior and development.

Clozapine—Sold under the brand name Clozaril, among others. It is an antipsychotic medication used for schizophrenia that does not improve, following the use of other antipsychotic medications.

Crisis Intervention Training—The CIT program is a first-responder model of police-based crisis intervention training to help persons with mental disorders and/or addictions access medical treatment rather than place them in the criminal justice system due to illness-related behaviors.

Depressive Episode—A period characterized by low mood and other depression symptoms that lasts for two weeks or more.

Dual Diagnosis—A person with dual diagnosis has both a mental disorder and an alcohol or drug problem. About half of people who have a mental disorder will also have a substance use disorder at some point in their lives, and vice versa.

ECO—An Emergency Custody Order is an order by a court authorizing a law enforcement agency to take a person into custody for a mental health evaluation performed by a qualified mental health clinician.

Family-To-Family—A free NAMI educational program for family, significant others, and friends of people with mental health conditions. It is a designated evidenced-based program.

HIPAA—The Health Insurance Portability and Accountability Act of 1996 required the Department of Health and Human Services (HHS) to develop regulations protecting the privacy and security of certain health information.

IMD Exclusion—The Medicaid Institutions for Mental Disease (IMD) exclusion is a federal rule which prohibits Medicaid payments to states for non-geriatric adults receiving psychiatric care in a treatment facility with more than 16 beds.

Lithium—A mood stabilizer medication that works in the brain. It is approved for the treatment of bipolar disorder.

LPS ACT—The Lanterman-Petris-Short Act is a California law governing the involuntary civil commitment of individuals who—due to mental illness—pose a danger to self, a danger to others, or who are gravely disabled and require inpatient psychiatric care.

Manic Depression—Former terminology for bipolar disorder.

NIH—National Institutes of Health is the largest biomedical research agency in the world.

NIMH—The National Institute of Mental Health is the lead federal agency for research on mental disorders

OCD—Obsessive-Compulsive Disorder is an anxiety disorder in which people have recurring, unwanted thoughts, ideas, or sensations (obsessions) that make them feel driven to do something repetitively (compulsions).

ODD—Oppositional Defiant Disorder is a type of behavior disorder. It is mostly diagnosed in childhood. Children with ODD are uncooperative, defiant, and hostile toward peers, parents, teachers, and other authority figures. They are more troubling to others than they are to themselves.

Olmstead Act—A United States Supreme Court decision that requires states to eliminate unnecessary segregation of persons with disabilities and to ensure that persons with disabilities receive services in the most integrated setting appropriate to their needs.

PAD—A psychiatric advance directive is a legal document that details a person's preferences for future mental health treatment, services, and supports, or names an individual to make treatment decisions should the person be in crisis and unable to make decisions.

Psychosis—A condition that affects the way a brain processes information and causes an individual to lose touch with reality. Psychosis is a symptom, not an illness.

PTSD—Post-Traumatic Stress Disorder is a mental health condition that's triggered by a terrifying event—either experiencing it or witnessing it. Symptoms may include flashbacks, nightmares, and severe anxiety, as well as uncontrollable thoughts about the event.

Schizoaffective Disorder—A mental health disorder marked by a combination of schizophrenia symptoms, such as hallucinations or delusions, and mood disorder symptoms, such as depression or mania.

Schizophrenia—A serious mental disorder in which people interpret reality abnormally. Schizophrenia may result in some combination of hallucinations, delusions, and extremely disordered thinking and behavior that impairs daily functioning, and can be disabling. People with schizophrenia require lifelong treatment.

Schizophrenoform Disorder—Is a type of psychotic illness with symptoms similar to those of schizophrenia, but lasting for less than six months.

Serious Mental Illness—SMI includes schizophrenia-spectrum disorders, severe bipolar disorder, and severe major depression. When other mental illnesses cause significant functional impairment and substantially limit major life activities, they also count as a serious mental illness.

SED—Children with Severe Emotional Disturbance are persons under the age of 18 who have a diagnosable mental, behavioral, or emotional disorder of significant duration. The disorder limits the child's functioning in family, school, or community activities.

5150—In the California Welfare and Insitutions Code, 5150 refers to an involuntary evaluation for persons deemed to have a mental disorder that makes them a danger to self and/or others, and/or is gravely disabled. Also known as a 72-hour hold.

5250—In the California Welfare and Insitutions Code, 5250 is known as a 14-day hold for persons alleged to meet the legal criteria of being a danger to self or others or being gravely disabled due to a mental disorder.

Acknowledgments

Thank you to the mothers/caregivers who contributed their stories to *Tomorrow Was Yesterday*.

Thank you to Judy Waldo Bracken and Mara Briere for proofreading the manuscript.

Thank you to Leslie Carpenter, Jerri Clark, and Laura Pogliano for text suggestions.

Thank you to Jim Moon for technical assistance.

Thank you to DJ Jaffe for your passionate, policy-based advocacy (1954–2020).

Thank you to 1106 Design for professionalism and guidance.

Thank you to *Tomorrow Was Yesterday* readers. Readers are the *why* in the *what if*.

Thank you to Patrick Ranahan. *Tomorrow Was Yesterday* is, in part, your legacy.

Thank you to SMI mothers/caregivers everywhere.

To help us disperse our stories far and wide,
please post a star rating and/or a review of

TOMORROW WAS YESTERDAY

on Amazon or any other book review website you prefer.
Thank you.

And if you want to help even more,
give a copy of this book to your political representatives,
or to your pastor, or to your therapist,
or to your next door neighbor, or to your best friend's mother.
Let's enlighten the world one person at a time.
Thank you again.

And, to keep this conversation going,
send your SMI stories to
Dede Ranahan at www.soonerthantomorrow.com
A Safe Place to Talk About Mental Illness in Our Families
Thank you one more time.

Sooner Than Tomorrow

Beautiful words with an undertone that has caught me . . . carrying me up and down. Such a good writer that I am grateful to be with you. I can borrow some courage here.

—JANET

Dede: Your writing is captivating. I find that I'm waiting for the next post, like when you finish a good novel and can't wait for the sequel. You and Pat have such a wonderful gift for using words in prose and poetry.

—JOAN A.

Thanks for sharing your life, Dede. Seven years after Josh's first psychotic break and two-and-a-half years after he ended his life in the hell of prison where he never should have been, I am still angry and heartbroken. I don't want anyone to suffer like Josh and we have. But there's some small comfort in knowing I'm not alone in the sadness that weighs me down everyday.

—ANNE

Dede, you amaze me with your writing ability and your candor in the face of major obstacles. Kiss the cat for me. I will kiss my dog in return.

—NANCY

Dede, you are such a good writer and have so much to say. Mental illness is a huge problem and getting worse every day. We see it in the many homeless people who live here in Medford.

—BETTE

Dede, I am so enjoying your story. So rich and naked.

—LINDA

I see the intelligence and the illness in Pat's posts. He made me laugh—but also evident is the stress on you. I hope you realize what a gem you have in that diary you kept. Pat really comes alive. I can hear his voice.

—CHRIS

I like the way you've included some funny stories with the thoughtful and frustrating stories. I feel like I can relate to your life, Dede. If this was your purpose, then you've succeeded in writing an engrossing and moving memoir.

—JAN M.

You are a stunning writer. Understatement makes many times more horrible. Awesome—awful, real, deep . . . must read. Beyond heartbreaking, my friend.

—SWANNIE

I love *Sooner Than Tomorrow*. Love it even though sometimes it makes me cry.

—JEAN

I read your latest post, and it's beautifully written. I don't say that lightly.

—RITA

So happy for the readers who will discover you.

—LIZ

I loved your diary entries today and laughed out loud several times.

—J.M.

Dede Ranahan graciously shares her story with us and it is absolutely amazing.

—MARY S.

I can relate to you and your son, Pat. I wish I'd written a journey on Shane but had no idea that I would outlive my son or that I would lose him at 39. Savor your time with your family. Even the difficult times.

—DARLENE

I love how you write—I hear your voice as I read your words.

—SHARON L.

Dede, So many of us thank you for continuing your advocacy work. How brave of you to continue the fight after losing Pat. Hope you receive the highest honors for *A Mother's Diary*.

—KIMBERLEE W.

Good reading.

—CRAIG W., HAWAII

The heartbreaking scenarios you describe here sound so very familiar. Thank you for your eloquent writing. I hope that everyone will read your book when it's published.

—MARILYN M.

Your writing skills are exceptional and I particularly love the way you string words together.

—V.

Dede, every one of your blog posts has a portion that I love so much that I take a screen shot and read it over and over. Your last blog had the reference to the grocery cart, and I used it in my company newsletter. This week my screen shot was your poem, which I will share with my grandkids.

—STACEY

I have always respected your writing talent and now coupled with such an important cause. The way you have turned your own personal tragedy into helping others is remarkable.

—PAM R.

I so much like to share your life. Sometimes I see me. I want more, more, more. So mark my name as an avid reader. How I would have loved to converse with Patrick. Such wonderful people in the world. Pity we don't know each other.

—GRANNAANNA

Thanks for your postings, Dede. They make us think.

—IRENE U.

Dede, I anxiously await each posting from your blog/book. You write with such skill, and not easy when it's so personal, but your passion sprinkled with humor are the reasons that this is successful.

—JOAN L.

Hi there, I just wanted to reach out and say thank you. I found your site through FB and the "kismet" is right there. In two weeks I am heading up to a monthly writers group here in Los Angeles. We will be writing about our experiences and emotions. It will be cathartic and healing and I've just sent a link of your site to everyone, to get inspired.

—K.

Best.ever.comment: "Trying to find meaning in the suffering . . . rising each day . . . no matter what."

—NANCY D.

I've done this, the primal scream and the mother animal instinct. There can't be anything more painful, not even death. My son was a normal little boy and a normal young man until schizophrenia came calling. Now I feel so shattered. I love your your diary.

—J.H.D.

Your wonderful Pat was blessed with a beautiful, caring, intelligent, and empathetic mother. From a kindred spirit and mama warrior.

—M.B.

Wow.

—R.K.

I think it's a special kind of talent you have in making people feel what you write. I hope you continue using your writing skills to paint the picture of what life is like for many people with SMI and their loved ones.

—CHANNIN H.W.

I love you, and I have grown to love your son, Pat, as well. It's a part of why I cherish the diary. The other reason is because you speak from your heart, the grief, the anguish, and the love that I feel for my son, Masai, too. Crying with you.

—TAMA B.

Dede, you have put words to heartbreaking loss and frustration with our system failure like no one else.

—JOYCE H.

Keep up the good work on your brilliant diary. When is it coming out in book form, please? I would love a copy.

—DEN P., UNITED KINGDOM

I can so relate to what you and the rest of us mothers are dealing with every day. Twenty-two years for me and it just gets worse year by year.

—DALE P-M.

If only this was all contrived drama. It's so visceral. You're an artist. "I didn't know, as I was writing, that I was capturing the last year of my son's life." This breaks my heart.

—HEIDI F.

Confidential To Patrick Ranahan

Akamai777, my son.
I love you forever.

—MOM